party popcorn

75 creative recipes
for everyone's favorite snack

ashton epps swank
photography by jason wyche

Houghton Mifflin Harcourt
Boston New York 2014

Copyright © 2014 by Ashton Swank
Photography © 2014 by Jason Wyche
A Hollan Publishing, Inc. Concept
Food styling by Chelsea Zimmer / Prop styling by Kira Corbin

For information about permission to reproduce selections
from this book, write to Permissions, Houghton Mifflin
Harcourt Publishing Company, 215 Park Avenue South,
New York, New York 10003.

www.hmhco.com

Library of Congress Cataloging-in-Publication Data
Swank, Ashton.
Party popcorn : 75 creative recipes for everyone's favorite snack / Ashton
Swank ; photography by Jason Wyche.
pages cm Includes index.
ISBN 978-0-544-22223-6 (hardback);
978-0-544-22202-1 (ebk)1. Cooking (Popcorn) I. Title.
TX814.5.P66S82 2014641.6'5677—dc232014001913

Printed in China
TOP 10 9 8 7 6 5 4 3 2 1

I looked out the
window and what did I see?
Popcorn popping
on the apricot tree.

—for Emma

table of contents

introduction

I am a stay-at-home-mom dessert blogger, and I am a firm believer in "do what you love, and love what you do." The beauty of blogging is that you can create and publish content completely based upon your own interests. Food has always been something I'm passionate about, regardless of blogging. I love the creativity I feel in mixing ingredients together to make something new. And I love the beauty I see in a smooth pool of melted chocolate or in a freshly baked cookie with all its buttery wrinkles and crinkles.

Popcorn is a special kind of food for the creative soul because it is the ultimate edible blank canvas. Everything about popcorn begs to be covered, smothered, drizzled, and sprinkled with something exciting and delicious. And that something could be *anything*. Popcorn has a subtle flavor, so it pairs well with sweet or savory ingredients, which leaves the door wide open for any number of flavor combinations.

Maybe more important than the versatility of popcorn are the warm and nostalgic feelings that accompany it. When I was a kid, it was a special treat to get popcorn at the movie theater. And even then, we had to share it among six siblings. My dad would line each of our cup holders with napkins and fill them with popcorn. It's silly, but as an adult I smile when I think about my dad roughly stuffing handfuls of popcorn into movie theater cup holders while his eagle-eyed children carefully watched to make sure all the portions were exactly the same.

When I was in college, my roommate taught me how to make Sea-Salted Caramel Corn (see page 55). As we made the popcorn, we giggled over boys and licked the caramel from our sticky fingers. We decided to hide half of the batch in a bag on top of the refrigerator to keep ourselves from eating all of it in one night. We succeeded in that endeavor, but we completely forgot about the popcorn until we found the bag three months later, when we were moving out of the apartment—which made us giggle all over again.

During the holiday season last year, I helped my two-year-old daughter make a popcorn garland for our Christmas tree. And I really couldn't tell you anything more particular about that memory if you asked me to, because it was just a simple moment. I was playing with popcorn with my daughter at Christmastime. And everything was lovely and perfect.

Popcorn, the food we snack on, is never the main attraction. It's something we bring along for the rides that are the most fun in life. We like to keep it with us for the big events and the little moments. And most of all, it's there for sharing with the people who will be making memories right alongside us.

recommendations, methods, and measurements

One of the many advantages to creating popcorn treats is that nothing has to be exact. Unlike baking, the chemistry involved in popcorn making is pretty minimal, which means you can "add a little here" or be "a little short on something there" without having catastrophic results. I am providing some basic measurement and method guidelines I used in developing the recipes in this book, but feel free to get creative and make adjustments as you go.

popping methods

AIR POPPING

This is my preferred popping method. Air poppers are available at most major retail stores and most are inexpensive. An air popper is just as easy to use as a microwave and, after the initial cost of the machine, is the most budget-friendly way to pop popcorn. I also love that air popping yields a popcorn with no additional flavors. This allows you to have complete control over the taste. Another great tidbit about air popping: You have total control over the amount of popcorn you make. You can simply pop a single-serving small batch, or you can decide you need a little more and throw another handful of kernels in the machine.

Follow the manufacturer's instructions to properly use your air-popping machine.

- ½ cup kernels yields approximately 8 cups popped popcorn

STOVETOP POPPING

Stovetop popping has many of the same benefits as air popping: It is also a very budget-friendly option and gives you a lot of control over the taste and quantity of the popcorn. However, it does require oil, constant attention during popping, and a little bit of elbow grease. The use of oil gives the popcorn a little bit of flavoring you don't get in air popping, but it's subtle and won't overwhelm other flavors in a recipe.

To pop popcorn on a stovetop, you'll need 1 tablespoon vegetable, canola, or coconut oil for ¼ cup kernels. Place the oil and one "test" kernel into a large, deep pot with a lid that fits comfortably on top. Heat the oil and the kernel over medium heat until the test kernel pops, 3 to 4 minutes. Once it has popped, add the remaining kernels to the pot and cover. Shake the pot back and forth over the burner continuously as the rest of the kernels pop (it may take a minute for the popping to start after you add the remaining kernels to the pot). Once the popping has stopped, remove the pot from the heat immediately so the popcorn on the bottom doesn't burn.

- ½ cup kernels yields approximately 8 cups popped popcorn

MICROWAVE POPPING

Let's face it: Sometimes the microwave is just the most feasible option for getting the job done. If using microwave popcorn is what works best for you, here are some tips for popping the best possible bag.

Buy natural or organic microwave popcorn because these options will have the least amount of flavoring in the bag. The flavors you will be adding with these recipes will taste much better than the "bag flavor," and you don't want your ingredients to be overwhelmed by the likes of imitation butter flavoring.

Buy fat-free or light popcorn if you can't find natural or organic. Again, these options will have very little flavoring in the bags.

Follow the popping instructions on the packaging.

Don't leave the popcorn alone in the microwave! Stand by while the bag is popping, and be sure to remove it when the popping has slowed to one pop every 3 seconds.

Be prepared with more bags of popcorn than a recipe may call for. It's not unusual to get a "dud" bag of microwave popcorn that does not yield as much popped popcorn as you are expecting.

Did you know that you can make your own microwave popcorn using a brown paper bag? It's one of my favorite lazy-day tricks because it offers all the convenience of a microwave but produces the clean, crisp taste of air-popped or stove-popped popcorn. See page 30 for my Brown Bag Microwave Popcorn.

- Two 3.5-ounce bags yield approximately 8 cups popped popcorn

popping measurements

In all the popping I did in preparation for this book, I have discovered there are no *exact* measurements in making popcorn. One tablespoon of kernels could yield a different amount for me in my kitchen than it does for you in yours. This could be caused simply by the quality of the kernels (not all kernels are equally up to the task of popping) or by various temperature conditions (the temperature of the machine, of the stove, or even of the room you are working in).

In the Popping Methods section above, I have provided approximate measurements applicable for most of the recipes in this book. However, keep in mind that actual measurements may be a little different for everyone depending on the kernels you use and the temperature they are popped at. The best way to find the right measurements for you and your kitchen will be to experiment with a batch or two.

melting candy

Melting candy—also called candy wafers, candy melts, and bark coating—is alternative chocolate or white chocolate coating used in candy and confection making. Many of the sweet recipes in this book call for melting candy instead of pure chocolates (which need to be tempered to properly set up and harden since they contain cocoa butter).

Melting candy is made specifically for coating purposes and is the optimal ingredient for coating popcorn. It melts quickly and smoothly, mixes well with other ingredients without seizing, easily coats, and will set up in less than thirty minutes. It doesn't melt on your fingers or rub off on packaging. Melting candy can be found in a variety of colors, and you can replace white candy coating with colored candy coating in any of the recipes in the book for a fun and colorful twist on your popcorn.

Chocolate and vanilla-flavored melting candies are widely available and can be found at most grocery stores. Here are some melting candy brands to look out for in the baking aisle or candy-making section of your grocery or craft store:

MILK CHOCOLATE
- Candiquik Candy Coating
- Ghirardelli Melting Wafers
- Hershey's Baking Melts
- Make 'n Mold Candy Wafers
- Merckens CK Confectionery Coating
- Nestlé Melts
- Plymouth Pantry Almond Bark
- Wilton Candy Melts

DARK CHOCOLATE
- Ghirardelli Melting Wafers
- Hershey's Baking Melts
- Make 'n Mold Candy Wafers
- Merckens CK Confectionery Coating
- Nestlé Melts
- Wilton Candy Melts

WHITE CHOCOLATE OR VANILLA
- Candiquik Candy Coating
- Ghirardelli Melting Wafers
- Make 'n Mold Candy Wafers
- Merckens CK Confectionery Coating
- Nestlé Melts
- Plymouth Pantry Almond Bark
- Wilton Candy Melts

COLORED
- Make 'n Mold Candy Wafers
- Merckens CK Confectionery Coating
- Wilton Candy Melts

measuring melting candy

When possible, select candy coating in wafer form instead of brick form. This will make it much easier to measure in recipes. If you must use candy coating in brick form, the easiest way to measure it will be to melt the entire brick and pour the amount you need into a measuring cup. Store the remaining coating in an airtight, microwave-safe container at room temperature. The next time you need candy coating, simply melt all the remaining coating in its container and once again pour only what you need. Candy coating can withstand being melted and cooled again several times with no adverse effects.

savory popcorn

nacho cheese doritos popcorn

SERVES: 4 TO 6

When I started creating popcorn recipes for this book, I decided to only use ingredients that could easily be found in most grocery stores. I didn't want people to get excited over a recipe but then be unable to find the ingredients. I knew I wanted to include some sort of nacho cheese popcorn, but cheese powder isn't an ingredient commonly found in most grocery stores—and who wants cheese powder anyway? So I decided instead to combine popcorn with an iconic nacho cheese snack food: Nacho Cheese Doritos.

8 cups popped popcorn (see page 7)
½ cup Nacho Cheese Doritos
½ teaspoon salt
4 tablespoons (½ stick) butter, melted

Pour the popcorn into a large bowl and remove any unpopped kernels.

Process the Doritos and salt in a food processor or blender until the Doritos become fine crumbs.

Drizzle the butter over the popcorn. Sprinkle with the Dorito crumbs and gently toss to coat. Serve immediately.

Prep time: 5 minutes
Cook time: 0 minutes
Cool time: 0 minutes

honey-mustard pretzel popcorn

SERVES: 4 TO 6

This version of honey-mustard popcorn is different from the typical honey-mustard snacks commonly seen at the grocery store. Instead of being doused in dry mustard, this popcorn is tossed with sourdough pretzel bites and coated in a honey-mustard syrup, then baked until crispy.

8 cups popped popcorn (see page 7)
1 cup sourdough pretzel bites
¾ cup packed light brown sugar
6 tablespoons yellow mustard
3 tablespoons honey
1 teaspoon dry mustard
¼ teaspoon baking soda

Preheat the oven to 300°F. Line a baking sheet with parchment paper or a silicone baking mat.

Pour the popcorn into a large bowl and remove any unpopped kernels. Add the pretzels to the bowl.

In a medium saucepan over medium heat, stir together the brown sugar, yellow mustard, honey, and dry mustard until the mixture reaches a slow bubble. Stop stirring and allow the mixture to boil for 4 minutes.

Remove from the heat immediately and mix in the baking soda (it will bubble up a bit).

Pour the honey-mustard mixture over the popcorn and pretzel bites. Using a large rubber spatula, gently stir to coat.

Spread the popcorn evenly onto the prepared baking sheet.

Bake the popcorn for 15 minutes.

Let cool in the pan for about 10 minutes before packaging or transferring to a bowl to serve immediately. The popcorn may be stored in an airtight container for up to 1 week.

Prep time: 10 minutes
Cook time: 15 minutes
Cool time: 10 minutes

sweet jalapeño barbecue popcorn

SERVES: 4 TO 6

My husband and I love to mix our favorite spicy flavors with something sweet and tangy. Jalapeños and barbecue sauce are a perfect combination. Sometimes we like to add bacon pieces, or even corn chips for a little Tex-Mex flavor.

8 cups popped popcorn (see page 7)
¾ cup packed light brown sugar
6 tablespoons barbecue sauce
3 tablespoons light corn syrup
2 jalapeños, seeded and sliced
¼ teaspoon baking soda

Preheat the oven to 300°F. Line a baking sheet with parchment paper or a silicone baking mat.

Pour the popcorn into a large bowl and remove any unpopped kernels.

In a medium saucepan over medium heat, stir together the brown sugar, barbecue sauce, and corn syrup until the mixture reaches a slow bubble. Stop stirring and allow the mixture to boil for 4 minutes.

Remove from the heat immediately and mix in the jalapeño slices and baking soda (the baking soda will bubble up a bit).

Pour the barbecue sauce mixture over the popcorn. Using a large rubber spatula, gently stir to coat.

Spread the popcorn evenly onto the prepared baking sheet.

Bake the popcorn for 15 minutes.

Let cool in the pan for about 10 minutes before transferring to a bowl to serve immediately.

Prep time: 10 minutes
Cook time: 15 minutes
Cool time: 10 minutes

coconut curry popcorn

SERVES: 4 TO 6

I'm obsessed with Thai curry dishes, so I was really thrilled with the success of this recipe. This fusion of Thai flavors with an all-American snack brings a little culture to movie food. Your friends are sure to be impressed.

8 cups popped popcorn (see page 7)
½ cup chopped cashews
½ cup sweetened flaked coconut
¼ cup coconut oil, melted (see Note)
1 tablespoon honey
1 tablespoon dried chives
1½ teaspoons curry powder
1 teaspoon salt
½ teaspoon granulated sugar

Pour the popcorn into a large bowl and remove any unpopped kernels. Add the cashews and coconut to the bowl.

Drizzle the coconut oil and honey over the popcorn. Gently toss to coat.

In a small bowl, mix together the chives, curry powder, salt, and sugar.

Sprinkle the curry mixture over the popcorn and gently toss to coat. Serve immediately.

NOTE: Using pure, unrefined coconut oil will lend a much stronger coconut flavor to the popcorn.

Prep time: 10 minutes
Cook time: 0 minutes
Cool time: 0 minutes

bacon ranch popcorn

SERVES: 4 TO 6

I love the simplicity of popcorn paired with a classic comfort-food flavor. I come from a long line of ranch dressing lovers, so this recipe is an obvious hands-down favorite for me.

8 cups popped popcorn (see page 7)
½ cup cooked bacon pieces (see Note)
1 tablespoon ranch dressing mix or ranch seasoning
½ teaspoon salt
4 tablespoons (½ stick) butter, melted

Pour the popcorn into a large bowl and remove any unpopped kernels. Add the bacon pieces to the bowl.

In a small bowl, mix together the ranch seasoning and salt.

Drizzle the butter over the popcorn. Sprinkle with the ranch seasoning mixture and gently toss to coat. Serve immediately.

NOTE: Instead of buying a bacon bits "product," cut up strips of real bacon. You can buy bacon strips already fully cooked, and the flavor and texture will be so much better than an imitation product.

Prep time: 5 minutes
Cook time: 0 minutes
Cool time: 0 minutes

buffalo ranch popcorn

SERVES: 4 TO 6

I mix Buffalo wing sauce and ranch dressing together as often as I possibly can. It makes an excellent dip for French fries, a tasty pizza sauce, and an amazing sandwich spread. It's no surprise that these two flavors come together so perfectly with popcorn. If you are sensitive to spicy flavors, just be sure to buy a mild Buffalo sauce (the creamy-looking sauces are usually less spicy). But if you're looking for a little flame, use an extra-spicy sauce, throw in a splash or two of hot sauce, and add a little ground cayenne pepper to the ranch seasoning. You'll have a fire on your hands in no time!

8 cups popped popcorn (see page 7)
2 tablespoons butter, melted
2 tablespoons Buffalo wing sauce
Half of a 1-ounce envelope ranch dressing mix or 1 tablespoon ranch seasoning
1 teaspoon salt

Pour the popcorn into a large bowl and remove any unpopped kernels.

In a small bowl, mix together the butter and Buffalo sauce. Drizzle over the popcorn and gently toss to coat.

Sprinkle the ranch seasoning and salt over the popcorn and gently toss to coat. Serve immediately.

Prep time: 5 minutes
Cook time: 0 minutes
Cool time: 0 minutes

bacon teriyaki popcorn

SERVES: 4 TO 6

This popcorn flavor is a surefire crowd pleaser at our house, and it won big gold stars from all my taste testers. I'm not much of a teriyaki gal myself (this popcorn flavor was inspired by my husband's taste), but even I found myself returning to the bowl again and again.

8 cups popped popcorn (see page 7)
¾ cup packed light brown sugar
6 tablespoons teriyaki sauce
3 tablespoons light corn syrup
½ cup cooked bacon pieces (see page 19)
¼ teaspoon baking soda

Preheat the oven to 300°F. Line a baking sheet with parchment paper or a silicone baking mat.

Pour the popcorn into a large bowl and remove any unpopped kernels.

In a medium saucepan over medium heat, stir together the brown sugar, teriyaki sauce, and corn syrup until the mixture reaches a slow bubble. Stop stirring and allow the mixture to boil for 4 minutes.

Remove from the heat immediately and stir in the bacon pieces. Mix in the baking soda (it will bubble up a bit).

Pour the teriyaki-bacon mixture over the popcorn. Using a large rubber spatula, gently stir to coat.

Spread the popcorn evenly onto the prepared baking sheet.

Bake the popcorn for 15 minutes.

Let cool in the pan for about 10 minutes before packaging or transferring to a bowl to serve immediately. The popcorn may be stored in an airtight container for up to 1 week.

Prep time: 10 minutes
Cook time: 15 minutes
Cool time: 10 minutes

mexican street corn popcorn

SERVES: 4 TO 6

I credit my husband and brother with the inspiration for this recipe. They both have ties to Mexican culture and love to eat corn on the cob smeared with mayonnaise and a paprika seasoning. I'll skip the mayo on my corn on the cob and take this popcorn twist on the Mexican street food instead. The lime in this popcorn really adds a fabulous dimension of flavor, and the cayenne pepper gives it the perfect kick.

8 cups popped popcorn (see page 7)
2 tablespoons butter, melted
2 tablespoons mayonnaise
1 teaspoon lime juice
1 teaspoon salt
1½ teaspoons paprika
¼ teaspoon granulated sugar
⅛ teaspoon ground cayenne pepper

Pour the popcorn into a large bowl and remove any unpopped kernels.

Whisk together the butter, mayonnaise, and lime juice in a small bowl. Drizzle over the popcorn and gently toss to coat.

In a small bowl, mix together the salt, paprika, sugar, and cayenne pepper. Sprinkle over the popcorn and gently toss to coat. Serve immediately.

Prep time: 10 minutes
Cook time: 0 minutes
Cool time: 0 minutes

pepperoni pizza popcorn

SERVES: 4 TO 6

As much as I love Parmesan cheese on my popcorn, I think I love an entire pizza on my popcorn even more. Classic pepperoni pizza ingredients added to a warm, buttery bowl of popcorn put a pretty extraordinary spin on pizza night. Get creative and see how some of your other favorite pizza toppings taste with this popcorn.

8 cups popped popcorn (see page 7)
½ cup pepperoni minis
¼ cup grated Parmesan cheese
1 tablespoon chopped fresh basil
1 teaspoon salt
4 tablespoons (½ stick) butter, melted
1 teaspoon red pepper flakes (optional)

Pour the popcorn into a large bowl, and make sure all of the unpopped kernals have been removed. Add the pepperoni to the bowl, and set aside.

Mix together the Parmesan cheese, basil, and salt in a small bowl.

Drizzle the butter over the popcorn and pepperoni. Sprinkle the Parmesan-basil mixture over the popcorn and gently toss to coat. Sprinkle with the red pepper flakes if using. Serve immediately.

Prep time: 5 minutes
Cook time: 0 minutes
Cool time: 0 minutes

sticky wings and blue cheese popcorn

SERVES: 4 TO 6

Many chicken wing restaurant chains carry some version of "sticky" wings on their menu, typically coated in a sweet and spicy sauce and utterly delicious. My husband and I love to make sticky wings at home, and the idea of turning our homemade sauce into a popcorn coating was too tempting not to try. The result? Phenomenal.

8 cups popped popcorn (see page 7)
6 tablespoons Buffalo wing sauce
3 tablespoons light corn syrup
2 tablespoons packed light brown sugar
½ teaspoon baking soda
½ cup crumbled blue cheese (see Note)

Preheat the oven to 300°F. Line a baking sheet with parchment paper or a silicone baking mat.

Pour the popcorn into a large bowl, and make sure all of the unpopped kernals have been removed.

In a medium saucepan over medium heat, stir together the Buffalo sauce, corn syrup, and brown sugar until the mixture reaches a slow bubble. Stop stirring and allow the mixture to boil for 4 minutes.

Remove from the heat immediately and mix in the baking soda (the baking soda will bubble up a bit).

Pour the Buffalo sauce mixture over the popcorn. Using a large rubber spatula, gently stir to coat.

Spread the popcorn evenly onto the prepared baking sheet and sprinkle with the crumbled blue cheese.

Bake the popcorn for 15 minutes.

Let cool in the pan for about 10 minutes before transferring to a bowl to serve immediately.

NOTE: The popcorn may be stored in an airtight container for up to 1 week if the crumbled blue cheese is omitted from the recipe.

Prep time: 10 minutes
Cook time: 15 minutes
Cool time: 10 minutes

pop 'n' toss popcorn

ready in five minutes
or less after popping

brown bag microwave popcorn

SERVES: 1

Using a brown paper bag and popcorn kernels is an excellent alternative to buying microwave popcorn bags. Not only does it save money, but it also keeps out unnecessary additive ingredients, giving you more control over the flavor of the popcorn.

3 tablespoons popcorn kernels
1 tablespoon butter, softened or melted
Pinch of salt

Place the kernels in a brown paper bag. Fold the top of the bag over three times.

Place the bag in the microwave standing upright. Microwave on medium power for 3 to 4 minutes, until the popping slows to a pop every 3 seconds.

Open the bag (see Note) and add the butter and salt. Refold the top of the bag and shake the bag to coat the popcorn. Eat immediately.

NOTE: Be careful of the steam escaping the bag when you first open it.

Prep time: 5 minutes
Cook time: 3 to 4 minutes
Cool time: 0 minutes

balsamic salt and vinegar popcorn

SERVES: 4 TO 6

After several failed attempts at a salt and vinegar recipe for this book, I finally tried using balsamic vinegar. It mixes really well with the butter, and as long as you take care to drizzle the mixture over the popcorn evenly (and not pour it all in one spot), the popcorn won't be soggy.

8 cups popped popcorn (see page 7)
2 tablespoons butter
1½ teaspoons balsamic vinegar
1 teaspoon coarse sea salt

Pour the popcorn into a large bowl and remove any unpopped kernels.

Place the butter and balsamic vinegar in a medium microwave-safe bowl. The mixture will bubble up, so the ingredients need to be in a bowl large enough to prevent the mixture from bubbling out of the bowl. Microwave on medium power for 30 to 60 seconds, until the butter is melted.

Whisk the butter and vinegar together in a small bowl.

Drizzle the butter-vinegar mixture over the popcorn. Sprinkle with the sea salt and gently toss to coat. Serve immediately.

Prep time: 5 minutes
Cook time: 0 minutes
Cool time: 0 minutes

basil garlic popcorn

SERVES: 4 TO 6

Fresh basil, garlic, and popcorn all have mouthwatering aromas. The only thing better than how they smell is, of course, how they taste. You can create all sorts of fun, fresh flavors with this recipe by using your favorite fresh herbs. Substituting cilantro for the fresh basil, for example, gives this popcorn a bold new flavor. If you're looking for something a little more subtle, try using dried herbs instead.

8 cups popped popcorn (see page 7)
1 tablespoon chopped fresh basil
3 tablespoons extra-virgin olive oil
1 teaspoon garlic salt

Pour the popcorn into a large bowl and remove any unpopped kernels. Add the basil to the bowl.

Drizzle the olive oil over the popcorn. Sprinkle with the garlic salt and gently toss to coat. Serve immediately.

Prep time: 5 minutes
Cook time: 0 minutes
Cool time: 0 minutes

olive oil and parmesan popcorn

SERVES 4 TO 6

The simplicity of this popcorn allows the flavors to really shine. The time you need for a quick drizzle, sprinkle, and toss is all the time you need to pull off this impressive bowl of popcorn.

8 cups popped popcorn (see page 7)
3 tablespoons extra-virgin olive oil
¼ cup grated Parmesan cheese
1 teaspoon Italian seasoning
1 teaspoon salt

Pour the popcorn into a large bowl and remove any unpopped kernels.

Drizzle the olive oil over the popcorn. Sprinkle with the Parmesan cheese, Italian seasoning, and salt and gently toss to coat. Serve immediately.

Prep time: 5 minutes
Cook time: 0 minutes
Cool time: 0 minutes

peppery lemon garlic popcorn

SERVES: 4 TO 6

Bringing these wonderful flavors together couldn't get any easier. Lemon pepper and garlic salt make this quick pop-and-toss recipe a no-brainer when you're looking for maximum flavor in minimum time.

8 cups popped popcorn (see page 7)
4 tablespoons (½ stick) butter, melted
2 teaspoons lemon pepper
1 teaspoon garlic salt

Pour the popcorn into a large bowl and remove any unpopped kernels.

Drizzle the butter over the popcorn. Sprinkle with the lemon pepper and garlic salt and gently toss to coat. Serve immediately.

Prep time: 5 minutes
Cook time: 0 minutes
Cool time: 0 minutes

taco lime popcorn

SERVES: 4 TO 6

Tacos and lime go together like peanut butter and jelly. Fortunately, taco seasoning and lime juice are simple ingredients that pack a powerful punch. Enjoy this delicious popcorn in less than a few minutes after popping.

8 cups popped popcorn (see page 7)
3 tablespoons butter, melted
1½ teaspoons lime juice
1 tablespoon taco seasoning

Pour the popcorn into a large bowl and remove any unpopped kernels. Whisk together the butter and lime juice in a small bowl.

Drizzle the butter-lime mixture over the popcorn. Sprinkle with the taco seasoning and gently toss to coat. Serve immediately.

Prep time: 5 minutes
Cook time: 0 minutes
Cool time: 0 minutes

cheesy ranch popcorn party mix

SERVES: 4 TO 6

Popcorn is making the scene with this fun and flavorful party mix. Cheese crackers, pretzels, and popcorn are drizzled in butter and tossed in ranch seasoning. No one will believe it took you less than five minutes to throw it together.

8 cups popped popcorn (see page 7)
½ cup small cheese crackers
½ cup mini pretzel twists
4 tablespoons (½ stick) butter, melted
1 tablespoon ranch dressing mix or ranch seasoning

Pour the popcorn into a large bowl and remove any unpopped kernels. Add the cheese crackers and pretzels to the bowl.

Drizzle the butter over the popcorn. Sprinkle with the ranch seasoning and gently toss to coat. Serve immediately.

Prep time: 5 minutes
Cook time: 0 minutes
Cool time: 0 minutes

cinnamon sugar popcorn

SERVES: 4 TO 6

When my husband and I make popcorn for our weeknight TV viewing, this recipe is always my pick. It may be simple, but it is absolutely perfect in every way. This popcorn drizzled in butter and tossed with cinnamon sugar hits the spot every time.

8 cups popped popcorn (see page 7)
¼ cup granulated sugar
1 teaspoon ground cinnamon
½ teaspoon salt
4 tablespoons (½ stick) butter, melted

Pour the popcorn into a large bowl and remove any unpopped kernels. In a small bowl, mix together the sugar, cinnamon, and salt.

Drizzle the butter over the popcorn. Sprinkle with the cinnamon sugar and gently toss to coat. Serve immediately.

Prep time: 5 minutes
Cook time: 0 minutes
Cool time: 0 minutes

salted honey-butter popcorn

SERVES: 4 TO 6

If it was a little more socially acceptable to eat honey butter with a spoon like ice cream, I am most certain that I would. Manners and a shred of social grace manage to restrain me, but not enough to keep me from drizzling honey butter over nearly everything I eat. Honey butter with a sprinkling of salt takes popcorn to a new level, and you may find it difficult to keep from diving into the bowl headfirst.

8 cups popped popcorn (see page 7)
4 tablespoons (½ stick) butter
¼ cup honey
1 teaspoon salt

Pour the popcorn into a large bowl and remove any unpopped kernels.

Place the butter and honey in a small microwave-safe bowl. Microwave on medium power for 30 seconds, until the butter is melted. Use a small whisk or fork to mix together the honey and butter.

Pour the honey butter over the popcorn. Sprinkle with the salt and gently toss to coat. Serve immediately.

Prep time: 5 minutes
Cook time: 0 minutes
Cool time: 0 minutes

cake batter popcorn

SERVES: 4 TO 6

Cake batter lovers, rejoice! This recipe is for you. It has all of the sweet taste of cake batter combined with the buttery goodness of popcorn. Add a splattering of rainbow-colored sprinkles for a delicious cakelike experience.

8 cups popped popcorn (see page 7)
5 tablespoons butter, melted
¼ cup yellow cake mix
1 teaspoon salt
1 tablespoon rainbow-colored sprinkles

Pour the popcorn into a large bowl and remove any unpopped kernels.

Whisk together the butter, cake mix, and salt in a small bowl. Drizzle over the popcorn. Using a large rubber spatula, gently stir to coat.

Sprinkle the sprinkles over the popcorn and serve immediately.

Prep time: 5 minutes
Cook time: 0 minutes
Cool time: 0 minutes

cran-apple cinnamon popcorn

SERVES: 4 TO 6

I have recently discovered my love for dried cranberries and just can't get enough of them. They add a tremendous burst of flavor to the popcorn and complement the apples in a wonderful way.

8 cups popped popcorn (see page 7)
½ cup dried apple pieces (chopped if the pieces are large)
½ cup dried cranberries
4 tablespoons (½ stick) butter, melted
¼ cup granulated sugar
1 teaspoon ground cinnamon
½ teaspoon salt

Pour the popcorn into a large bowl and remove any unpopped kernels. Add the dried apples and cranberries to the bowl.

In a small bowl, mix together the sugar, cinnamon, and salt.

Drizzle the butter over the popcorn. Sprinkle with the sugar mixture and gently toss to coat. Serve immediately.

Prep time: 5 minutes
Cook time: 0 minutes
Cool time: 0 minutes

quick marshmallow mix popcorn

SERVES: 4 TO 6

This is the quick version of my mom's Gooey Marshmallow Popcorn (see page 81). When I'm looking for the same flavors she brought to that recipe, but don't have the time or inclination to make a marshmallow coating, I turn to this simple and deliciously buttery alternative.

8 cups popped popcorn (see page 7)
1 cup miniature marshmallows
½ cup plain milk chocolate candies, miniature size
½ cup almonds, peanuts, or cashews
5 tablespoons butter, melted
1 teaspoon salt

Pour the popcorn into a large bowl and remove any unpopped kernels. Add the marshmallows, chocolate candies, and nuts to the bowl.

Drizzle the butter over the popcorn. Sprinkle with the salt and gently toss to coat. Serve immediately.

Prep time: 5 minutes
Cook time: 0 minutes
Cool time: 0 minutes

honey-roasted peanut popcorn

SERVES: 4 TO 6

Honey-roasted peanuts add a delicious crunch and flavor to popcorn drizzled in honey and butter. This popcorn is full of comfort-food flavors and is ready to go in just a few short minutes.

8 cups popped popcorn (see page 7)
2 tablespoons butter, melted
1 teaspoon salt
¼ cup honey
¼ cup honey-roasted peanuts

Pour the popcorn into a large bowl and remove any unpopped kernels.

Drizzle the butter over the popcorn. Sprinkle with the salt and gently toss to coat.

Drizzle the honey over the popcorn and add the peanuts. Gently toss again to coat. Serve immediately.

Prep time: 5 minutes
Cook time: 0 minutes
Cool time: 0 minutes

sweet popcorn

peanut butter cup popcorn

SERVES: 6

Peanut butter cups make the world go round. I couldn't write any sort of cookbook without including a recipe centered on these all-time favorite candy morsels. Enjoy an explosion of peanut butter and chocolate flavors in every delicious bite.

8 cups popped popcorn (see page 7)
1 cup milk chocolate melting candy (see page 9)
1 tablespoon peanut butter
½ cup miniature peanut butter cups, halved

Pour the popcorn into a large bowl and remove any unpopped kernels.

Place the chocolate melting candy and peanut butter in a medium microwave-safe bowl. Microwave on medium power for 1 minute. Stir until melted and smooth. If needed, add additional heating time in 30-second increments, stirring after each time, until the candy is melted and smooth.

Pour the melted candy over the popcorn. Add the peanut butter cups to the bowl. Using a large rubber spatula, gently stir to coat.

Spread the popcorn mixture on a large piece of parchment paper or a large silicone baking mat.

Allow to cool until the chocolate coating has hardened, about 20 minutes. Break into pieces before packaging or transferring to a bowl to serve immediately. The popcorn may be stored in an airtight container for up to 4 days.

Prep time: 10 minutes
Cook time: 0 minutes
Cool time: 20 minutes

muddy buddy popcorn

SERVES: 4 TO 6

Chocolate, peanut butter, confectioners' sugar, and popcorn: it's a combination bound to put a sugary smile on the face of everyone who gets a bite. Inspired by the classic cereal snack mix, also known as "puppy chow," this sweet snack hits the spot just right every time.

8 cups popped popcorn (see page 7)
1½ cups confectioners' sugar
¼ cup peanut butter
½ cup semisweet chocolate chips (see Note)
1 teaspoon vanilla extract

Pour the popcorn into a large bowl and remove any unpopped kernels. Place the confectioners' sugar in a gallon-size zip-top bag.

Place the peanut butter and chocolate chips in a medium microwave-safe bowl. Microwave on medium power for 1 minute or until the chocolate chips are melted. If needed, add additional heating time in 30-second increments, stirring after each time, until the chocolate and the peanut butter are melted and the mixture is smooth. Mix in the vanilla extract.

Pour the chocolate–peanut butter mixture over the popcorn. Using a large rubber spatula, gently stir to coat.

Spoon the coated popcorn into the prepared zip-top bag. Seal the bag and shake to coat the popcorn in the sugar.

Once the popcorn is coated, transfer to a bowl to serve immediately. The popcorn may be stored in an airtight container for up to 2 days.

NOTE: This is one of the few sweet recipes in this book that calls for chocolate chips instead of melting candy. Since you are coating the chocolate–peanut butter mixture in confectioners' sugar, there is no need to use a chocolate that will harden.

Prep time: 15 minutes
Cook time: 0 minutes
Cool time: 0 minutes

"everything but the kitchen sink" popcorn

SERVES: 6

You've heard the phrase "everything but the kitchen sink." In cooking, it means using everything you have on hand except for the kitchen sink (because we all know that thing isn't moving). That's exactly the idea behind this popcorn recipe. Swing open the pantry doors, break into the cookie jar, and dig out your candy stash! Find your favorite goodies and toss them into the popcorn bowl with white chocolate to create a fun, new, sweet snack mix every time you make it. Chocolate candies, chocolate chip cookies, and mixed nuts are some of my favorite ingredients to add to this popcorn, but feel free to mix things up and substitute your favorites instead.

8 cups popped popcorn (see page 7)
1 cup white chocolate or vanilla melting candy (see page 11)
½ cup plain milk chocolate candies, miniature size
½ cup crumbled chocolate chip cookies
½ cup mixed nuts

Pour the popcorn into a large bowl and remove any unpopped kernels.

Place the white melting candy in a medium microwave-safe bowl. Microwave on medium power for 1 minute. Stir until melted and smooth. If needed, add additional heating time in 30-second increments, stirring after each time, until the candy is melted and smooth.

Pour the melted candy over the popcorn, but do not stir yet.

Add the milk chocolate candies, chocolate chip cookies, and mixed nuts to the popcorn. Using a large rubber spatula, gently stir to coat.

Spread the popcorn mixture on a large piece of parchment paper or a large silicone baking mat.

Allow to cool until the candy coating has hardened, about 20 minutes. Break into pieces before packaging or transferring to a bowl to serve immediately. The popcorn may be stored in an airtight container for up to 4 days.

Prep time: 15 minutes
Cook time: 0 minutes
Cool time: 20 minutes

sea-salted caramel corn

SERVES: 6

A sprinkling of sea salt adds a depth of flavor to the caramel in this recipe, and it has become a movie night staple in our home. If you want to get a little fancy, dress it up with a chocolate drizzle.

8 cups popped popcorn (see page 7)
¾ cup packed light brown sugar
6 tablespoons (¾ stick) butter
3 tablespoons light corn syrup
½ teaspoon vanilla extract
¼ teaspoon baking soda
1½ teaspoons coarse sea salt

Preheat the oven to 300°F. Line a baking sheet with parchment paper or a silicone baking mat.

Pour the popcorn into a large bowl and remove any unpopped kernels.

In a medium saucepan over medium heat, stir together the brown sugar, butter, and corn syrup until the butter has melted and the mixture reaches a slow bubble. Allow the mixture to boil for 4 minutes.

Remove from the heat immediately and mix in the vanilla extract and baking soda (the baking soda will bubble up a bit).

Pour the caramel mixture over the popcorn. Using a large rubber spatula, gently stir to coat.

Spread the popcorn evenly onto the prepared baking sheet and sprinkle with the sea salt, adding more to taste if desired.

Bake the popcorn for 10 to 15 minutes. A 10-minute bake will yield a chewy caramel corn (see Note), while a 15-minute bake will yield a crunchy caramel corn.

Let cool in the pan for about 10 minutes before transferring to a bowl and serving.

Serve chewy caramel popcorn immediately. Crunchy caramel popcorn may be stored in an airtight container for up to 1 week. Let cool completely before packaging.

NOTE: I love eating this popcorn chewy. But if I'm planning on giving it away, I always make it crunchy so that it is easier to package and will have a longer shelf life.

Prep time: 10 minutes
Cook time: 10 to 15 minutes
Cool time: 10 minutes

german chocolate cake popcorn

SERVES: 6

One of the great things about German chocolate cake is that it seems so fancy, but it can actually be so simple to make. This popcorn has all the taste and appearance of a complicated recipe, but in reality it couldn't be easier.

8 cups popped popcorn (see page 7)
3 plain chocolate cupcakes or muffins (no frosting; see Note)
¾ cup packed light brown sugar
6 tablespoons (¾ stick) butter
3 tablespoons light corn syrup
½ teaspoon vanilla extract
¼ teaspoon baking soda
½ cup sweetened flaked coconut
½ cup pecan halves

Preheat the oven to 300°F. Line a baking sheet with parchment paper or a silicone baking mat.

Pour the popcorn into a large bowl and remove any unpopped kernels. Crumble the chocolate cupcakes over the popcorn (large pieces are desirable, so don't crumble them up too much).

In a medium saucepan over medium heat, stir together the brown sugar, butter, and corn syrup until the butter has melted and the mixture reaches a slow bubble. Stop stirring and allow the mixture to boil for 4 minutes.

Remove from the heat immediately and mix in the vanilla extract and baking soda (the baking soda will bubble up a bit). Stir in the coconut and pecan halves.

Pour the caramel mixture over the popcorn and cake pieces. Using a large rubber spatula, gently stir to coat.

Spread the popcorn evenly onto the prepared baking sheet.

Bake the popcorn for 10 minutes.

Let cool in the pan for about 10 minutes before transferring to a bowl to serve immediately.

NOTE: Plain chocolate cupcakes or muffins can usually be found in the grocery store bakery.

Prep time: 15 minutes
Cook time: 10 minutes
Cool time: 10 minutes

lemon cream pie popcorn

SERVES: 6

Lemon cream pie isn't just for plates and forks anymore. You can eat pie by the fistful when you bring pie and popcorn together in this recipe.

8 cups popped popcorn (see page 7)
1 cup white chocolate or vanilla melting candy (see page 11)
2 teaspoons lemon-flavored instant pudding mix (see Note)
4 graham crackers

Pour the popcorn into a large bowl and remove any unpopped kernels.

Place the white melting candy in a medium microwave-safe bowl. Microwave on medium power for 1 minute. Stir until melted and smooth. If needed, add additional heating time in 30-second increments, stirring after each time, until the candy is melted and smooth. Whisk the pudding mix into the melting candy.

Pour the melted candy over the popcorn, but do not stir yet.

Crumble the graham crackers into the popcorn bowl. Using a large rubber spatula, gently stir to coat.

Spread the popcorn mixture on a large piece of parchment paper or a large silicone baking mat.

Allow to cool until the candy coating has hardened, about 20 minutes. Break into pieces before packaging or transferring to a bowl to serve immediately. The popcorn may be stored in an airtight container for up to 4 days.

NOTE: The pudding mix will not change the color of the candy coating to a bright lemon yellow. If you want the coating to be colored, use yellow-colored melting candy instead of white melting candy (see page 11).

Prep time: 10 minutes
Cook time: 0 minutes
Cool time: 20 minutes

grasshopper popcorn

SERVES: 6

Chocolate, mint, and fudge-covered cookies make this popcorn an irresistible snack. The flavors work perfectly with the popcorn, but the real treat is the combination of crunchy chocolate cookies with the crispy popcorn. Package this popcorn in sweet little bags with a note that says, "This popcorn was 'mint' just for you!"

8 cups popped popcorn (see page 7)
One 10-ounce package fudge mint cookies
1 cup milk chocolate melting candy (see page 9)
1 cup Andes Crème de Menthe Baking Chips

Pour the popcorn into a large bowl and remove any unpopped kernels. Roughly chop the cookies into small pieces.

Place the chocolate melting candy in a medium microwave-safe bowl. Microwave on medium power for 1 minute. Stir until melted and smooth. If needed, add additional heating time in 30-second increments, stirring after each time, until the candy is melted and smooth.

Pour the melted candy over the popcorn, but do not stir yet.

Add the chopped cookies and the baking chips to the popcorn bowl. Using a large rubber spatula, gently stir to coat.

Spread the popcorn mixture on a large piece of parchment paper or a large silicone baking mat.

Allow to cool until the chocolate coating has hardened, about 20 minutes. Break into pieces before packaging or transferring to a bowl to serve immediately. The popcorn may be stored in an airtight container for up to 4 days.

Prep time: 10 minutes
Cook time: 0 minutes
Cool time: 20 minutes

chocolate crispy candy bar popcorn

SERVES: 6

This popcorn reminds me of Halloween night as a kid, after the trick-or-treating, when you're sitting around sorting out the candy. The only candy bars I ever wanted were the chocolate crispy candy bars. I would trade my entire bucket for everyone else's stash of those little candy bars. They're still one of my favorite treats, and I love getting to bring the taste of those candy bars to a bowl of popcorn.

8 cups popped popcorn (see page 7)
1 cup milk chocolate melting candy (see page 9)
1 cup puffed rice cereal

Pour the popcorn into a large bowl and remove any unpopped kernels.

Place the chocolate melting candy in a medium microwave-safe bowl. Microwave on medium power for 1 minute. Stir until melted and smooth. If needed, add additional heating time in 30-second increments, stirring after each time, until the candy is melted and smooth.

Pour the melted candy over the popcorn, but do not stir yet.

Add the puffed rice cereal to the popcorn bowl. Using a large rubber spatula, gently stir to coat.

Spread the popcorn mixture on a large piece of parchment paper or a large silicone baking mat.

Allow to cool until the chocolate coating has hardened, about 20 minutes. Break into pieces before packaging or transferring to a bowl to serve immediately. The popcorn may be stored in an airtight container for up to 4 days.

Prep time: 10 minutes
Cook time: 0 minutes
Cool time: 20 minutes

scotcheroos **popcorn**

SERVES: 6

Scotcheroos are a type of crispy cereal bar made with butterscotch chips and peanut butter and drizzled with chocolate. They are a bit sticky and chewy and are utterly delicious and unforgettable, as is this popcorn.

8 cups popped popcorn (see page 7)
¾ cup butterscotch chips (see Note)
3 tablespoons peanut butter
¼ cup milk chocolate melting candy (see page 9)

Pour the popcorn into a large bowl and remove any unpopped kernels.

Place the butterscotch chips and peanut butter in a 2-quart saucepan over medium-low heat. Stir until smooth and melted (this may take 8 to 10 minutes). Remove from the heat immediately.

Pour the butterscotch–peanut butter mixture over the popcorn. Using a large rubber spatula, gently stir to coat.

Spread the popcorn mixture on a large piece of parchment paper or a large silicone baking mat.

Place the chocolate melting candy in a small microwave-safe bowl. Microwave on medium power for 30 seconds. Stir until melted and smooth. If needed, heat for an additional 30 seconds.

Transfer the chocolate to a zip-top bag or piping bag. Press all the air out of the bag and snip the corner off. Use this bag to drizzle the chocolate across the popcorn.

Allow to cool until the chocolate drizzle has hardened, about 20 minutes. Transfer to a bowl to serve immediately.

NOTE: I have rarely been able to find melting candy in butterscotch flavor, which is why this recipe calls for butterscotch chips instead of melting candy. Using the chips means that the popcorn will not set up and harden completely. But the flavor of this popcorn is so good that it's worth the sticky fingers.

Prep time: 5 minutes
Cook time: 10 minutes
Cool time: 20 minutes

avalanche popcorn

SERVES: 6

One of our favorite dates to go on as a newly married couple was a walk to a nearby chocolatier where we would buy and split an "avalanche" candy apple. The apple was dipped in a peanut butter–white chocolate coating, sprinkled with crispy rice cereal and miniature marshmallows, and drizzled with milk chocolate. That apple inspired this popcorn, and now we love eating it when we stay home for date night.

> 8 cups popped popcorn (see page 7)
> 1 cup white chocolate or vanilla melting candy (see page 11)
> 3 tablespoons peanut butter
> ½ cup puffed rice cereal
> ½ cup miniature marshmallows
> ¼ milk chocolate melting candy (see page 9)

Pour the popcorn into a large bowl and remove any unpopped kernels.

Place the white melting candy and peanut butter in a medium microwave-safe bowl. Microwave on medium power for 1 minute. Stir until melted and smooth. If needed, add additional time in 30-second increments, stirring after each time, until the candy is melted and smooth.

Pour the chocolate–peanut butter mixture over the popcorn, but do not stir yet.

Add the puffed rice cereal and marshmallows to the popcorn bowl. Using a large rubber spatula, gently stir to coat.

Spread the popcorn mixture on a large piece of parchment paper or a large silicone baking mat.

Place the milk chocolate melting candy in a small microwave-safe bowl. Microwave on medium power for 30 seconds. Stir until melted and smooth. If needed, heat for an additional 30 seconds.

Transfer the chocolate to a zip-top bag or piping bag. Press all the air out of the bag and snip the corner off. Use this bag to drizzle the chocolate across the popcorn.

Allow to cool until the candy coating has hardened, about 20 minutes. Break into pieces before packaging or transferring to a bowl to serve immediately. The popcorn may be stored in an airtight container for up to 4 days.

Prep time: 15 minutes
Cook time: 0 minutes
Cool time: 20 minutes

maple bacon popcorn

SERVES: 4 TO 6

Together, maple and bacon are classic, charming, and timeless. The flavors remind us of waking up to sweet aromas, breakfasts in bed, and big, warm hugs. Creative cooks have unleashed maple and bacon from simply being breakfast flavors, and these days you can find the dynamic duo on fried chicken, in breads, and, now, in your popcorn.

8 cups popped popcorn (see page 7)
¾ cup packed light brown sugar
6 tablespoons (¾ stick) butter
3 tablespoons maple syrup
½ teaspoon maple extract
¼ teaspoon baking soda
½ cup cooked bacon pieces (see page 19)
1½ teaspoons coarse sea salt

Preheat the oven to 300°F. Line a baking sheet with parchment paper or a silicone baking mat.

Pour the popcorn into a large bowl and remove any unpopped kernels.

In a medium saucepan over medium heat, stir together the brown sugar, butter, and maple syrup until the butter has melted and the mixture reaches a slow bubble. Stop stirring and allow the mixture to boil for 4 minutes.

Remove from the heat immediately and mix in the maple extract and baking soda (the baking soda will bubble up a bit). Stir in the bacon pieces.

Pour the maple syrup–bacon mixture over the popcorn. Using a large rubber spatula, gently stir to coat.

Spread the popcorn evenly onto the prepared baking sheet and sprinkle with the sea salt, adding more to taste if desired.

Bake the popcorn for 10 to 15 minutes. A 10-minute bake will yield a chewy popcorn, while a 15-minute bake will yield a crunchy popcorn.

Let cool in the pan for about 10 minutes before transferring to a bowl to serve immediately.

Prep time: 10 minutes
Cook time: 10 to 15 minutes
Cool time: 10 minutes

chocolate-covered potato chip popcorn

SERVES: 6

Sweet and salty is one of my favorite pairings, and I am especially partial to chocolate-covered potato chips. I've brought that fun treat to popcorn, and I just know you're going to love this combination as much as I do.

8 cups popped popcorn (see page 7)
1 cup milk chocolate melting candy (see page 9)
1 cup potato chips with ridges
½ teaspoon coarse sea salt

Pour the popcorn into a large bowl and remove any unpopped kernels.

Place the chocolate melting candy in a medium microwave-safe bowl. Microwave on medium power for 1 minute. Stir until melted and smooth. If needed, add additional heating time in 30-second increments, stirring after each time, until the candy is melted and smooth.

Pour the melted candy over the popcorn, but do not stir yet.

Crumble the potato chips over the popcorn bowl (it is okay to have big pieces). Using a large rubber spatula, gently stir to coat.

Spread the popcorn mixture on a large piece of parchment paper or a large silicone baking mat, and sprinkle with the sea salt, adding more to taste if desired.

Allow to cool until the chocolate coating has hardened, about 20 minutes. Break into pieces before packaging or transferring to a bowl to serve immediately. The popcorn may be stored in an airtight container for up to 4 days.

Prep time: 10 minutes
Cook time: 0 minutes
Cool time: 20 minutes

chocolate-hazelnut popcorn

SERVES: 6

I don't know if there's an ingredient I love more than chocolate-hazelnut spread. I think I like it best on a spoon straight out of the jar, but if I absolutely have to part ways with spoon-feeding it to myself, adding chocolate-hazelnut spread to popcorn seems like an acceptable alternative. This way I can skip the spoon and simply eat it by the handful.

8 cups popped popcorn (see page 7)
1 cup milk chocolate melting candy (see page 9)
3 tablespoons chocolate-hazelnut spread
2 ounces hazelnuts, chopped, divided

Pour the popcorn into a large bowl and remove any unpopped kernels.

Place the chocolate melting candy and chocolate-hazelnut spread in a medium microwave-safe bowl. Microwave on medium power for 1 minute. Stir until melted and smooth. If needed, add additional heating time in 30-second increments, stirring after each time, until the candy is melted and smooth.

Pour the melted candy over the popcorn, but do not stir yet.

Reserving 2 tablespoons for garnish, add the chopped hazelnuts to the popcorn bowl. Using a large rubber spatula, gently stir to coat.

Spread the popcorn mixture on a large piece of parchment paper or a large silicone baking mat. Sprinkle the remaining chopped hazelnuts over the popcorn.

Allow to cool until the chocolate coating has hardened, about 20 minutes. Break into pieces before packaging or transferring to a bowl to serve immediately. The popcorn may be stored in an airtight container for up to 4 days.

Prep time: 10 minutes
Cook time: 0 minutes
Cool time: 20 minutes

caramel apple crisp popcorn

SERVES: 6

Caramel apple crisp is the perfect dessert for heralding in the fall. It's warm and rich and decadent. Its deep cinnamon fragrance is warm and inviting and beckons you to do things like cuddle and read old books. Fill a popcorn bowl with all of that and you'll have a cozy snack that will have you curled up with a blanket and your favorite book in no time.

8 cups popped popcorn (see page 7)
¾ cup packed light brown sugar
6 tablespoons (¾ stick) butter
3 tablespoons light corn syrup
½ teaspoon vanilla extract
½ teaspoon ground cinnamon
¼ teaspoon baking soda
½ cup dried apple pieces (chopped if the pieces are large)
½ cup granola cereal

Preheat the oven to 300°F. Line a baking sheet with parchment paper or a silicone baking mat.

Pour the popcorn into a large bowl and remove any unpopped kernels.

In a medium saucepan over medium heat, stir together the brown sugar, butter, and corn syrup until the butter has melted and the mixture reaches a slow bubble. Stop stirring and allow the mixture to boil for 4 minutes.

Remove from the heat immediately and mix in the vanilla extract, cinnamon, and baking soda (the baking soda will bubble up a bit). Stir in the dried apple pieces and granola cereal.

Pour the caramel-apple mixture over the popcorn. Using a large rubber spatula, gently stir to coat.

Spread the popcorn evenly onto the prepared baking sheet.

Bake the popcorn for 15 minutes.

Let cool in the pan for about 10 minutes before packaging or transferring to a bowl to serve immediately. The popcorn may be stored in an airtight container for up to 1 week.

Prep time: 10 minutes
Cook time: 15 minutes
Cool time: 10 minutes

turtle brownie popcorn

SERVES: 6

This crispy popcorn is a decadent treat perfect for gift giving. Everyone wants a big bag full of brownies, pecans, chocolate, and popcorn all coated in a crispy caramel coating. The only problem with this recipe is that no matter how much you make, there is never, ever enough.

8 cups popped popcorn (see page 7)
¾ cup packed light brown sugar
6 tablespoons (¾ stick) butter
3 tablespoons light corn syrup
½ teaspoon vanilla extract
¼ teaspoon baking soda
1 cup milk chocolate melting candy (see page 9)
½ cup crumbled brownies (see Note)
½ cup pecan halves

Preheat the oven to 300°F. Line a baking sheet with parchment paper or a silicone baking mat.

Pour the popcorn into a large bowl and remove any unpopped kernels.

In a medium saucepan over medium heat, stir together the brown sugar, butter, and corn syrup until the butter has melted and the mixture reaches a slow bubble. Stop stirring and allow the mixture to boil for 4 minutes.

Remove from the heat immediately and mix in the vanilla extract and baking soda (the baking soda will bubble up a bit).

Pour the caramel mixture over the popcorn. Using a large spatula, gently stir to coat.

Spread the popcorn evenly onto the prepared baking sheet.

Bake the popcorn for 15 minutes.

Let cool in the pan for about 10 minutes before transferring to a bowl. Break the popcorn into pieces.

Place the chocolate melting candy in a medium microwave-safe bowl. Microwave on medium power for 1 minute. Stir until melted and smooth. If needed, add additional heating time in 30-second increments, stirring after each time, until the candy is melted and smooth.

Pour the melted candy over the popcorn, but do not stir yet. Add the crumbled brownies and pecan halves to the bowl. Using a large spatula, gently stir to coat.

Spread the popcorn mixture on a large piece of parchment paper or a large silicone baking mat.

Allow to cool until the chocolate coating has hardened, about 20 minutes. Break into pieces before packaging or transferring to a bowl to

serve immediately. The popcorn may be stored in an airtight container for up to 1 week.

NOTE: You can use store-bought brownie bites for this recipe unless you happen to have leftover brownies just lying around.

Prep time: 10 minutes
Cook time: 15 minutes
Cool time: 20 minutes

orange cream popcorn

SERVES: 6

Orange Creamsicle is one of my husband's favorite
dessert flavors, and I can't say that I blame him. The flavor
is so light and easy to keep munching on. This recipe uses
gelatin mix to give the white candy coating an orange
flavor, which has a tang that I really like.

8 cups popped popcorn (see page 7)
½ cup miniature marshmallows
1 cup white chocolate or vanilla melting candy (see page 11)
1 teaspoon orange-flavored instant gelatin mix (see Note)

Pour the popcorn into a large bowl and remove any unpopped kernels.
Add the marshmallows to the bowl.

Place the white melting candy in a medium microwave-safe bowl.
Microwave on medium power for 1 minute. Stir until melted and smooth.
If needed, add additional heating time in 30-second increments, stirring
after each time, until the candy is melted and smooth. Whisk the gelatin
mix into the melting candy.

Pour the melted candy over the popcorn. Using a large rubber spatula,
gently stir to coat.

Spread the popcorn mixture on a large piece of parchment paper or a
large silicone baking mat.

Allow to cool until the candy coating has hardened, about 20 minutes.
Break into pieces before packaging or transferring to a bowl to serve
immediately. The popcorn may be stored in an airtight container for up to
4 days.

NOTE: The gelatin mix will not change the color of the candy coating to a bright
orange. If you want the coating to be colored, use orange-colored melting candy
instead of white melting candy (see page 11).

Prep time: 10 minutes
Cook time: 0 minutes
Cool time: 20 minutes

cinnamon roll popcorn

SERVES: 6

The idea behind this recipe was to take all the components
of a cinnamon roll (cinnamon, brown sugar, butter, cream
cheese frosting) and turn them into a popcorn recipe.
I went through a few different versions before finally
settling on this recipe, which ended up being the simplest
arrangement of the ingredients I had tried. Sometimes it's
the simple things that turn out the greatest.

8 cups popped popcorn (see page 7)
¼ cup packed light brown sugar
1 teaspoon ground cinnamon
½ teaspoon salt
3 tablespoons canned cream cheese frosting

Pour the popcorn into a large bowl and remove any unpopped kernels.
In a small bowl, mix together the brown sugar, cinnamon, and salt.
Place the canned cream cheese frosting in a small microwave-safe bowl.
Microwave on medium power for 30 seconds or until melted. Stir until the
frosting is smooth and has an even consistency.

Drizzle the melted frosting over the popcorn. Sprinkle with the brown
sugar mixture. Using a large rubber spatula, gently stir to coat. Serve
immediately.

Prep time: 5 minutes
Cook time: 0 minutes
Cool time: 0 minutes

peanut butter–
chocolate chip popcorn

SERVES: 6

Peanut butter and chocolate seem to be an all-time favorite flavor among the masses. Anytime I post a peanut butter and chocolate recipe on my blog, the world goes crazy for it. Never mind the eight hundred other recipes I've posted. "We want peanut butter and chocolate!" they say. And who am I to say no?

8 cups popped popcorn (see page 7)
1 cup white chocolate or vanilla melting candy (see page 11)
3 tablespoons peanut butter
½ cup mini chocolate chips

Pour the popcorn into a large bowl and remove any unpopped kernels.

Place the white melting candy and peanut butter in a medium microwave-safe bowl. Microwave on medium power for 1 minute. Stir until melted and smooth. If needed, add additional heating time in 30-second increments, stirring after each time, until the candy is melted and smooth.

Pour the melted candy over the popcorn. Using a large rubber spatula, gently stir to coat.

Spread the popcorn mixture on a large piece of parchment paper or a large silicone baking mat. Sprinkle the chocolate chips over the popcorn.

Allow to cool until the candy coating has hardened, about 20 minutes. Break into pieces before packaging or transferring to a bowl to serve immediately. The popcorn may be stored in an airtight container for up to 4 days.

Prep time: 10 minutes
Cook time: 0 minutes
Cool time: 20 minutes

pistachio popcorn

SERVES: 6

I love pistachios for their surprising flavor. Up front, they taste a lot like any other nut. That is, until their sweetness sneaks up from behind and takes you by surprise. It's this unique blend of nutty and sweet that makes a pistachio so special. I particularly love pistachios with chocolate. It's a delicious pairing and also one that is as beautiful as it is tasty. Sprinkle some chopped pistachios on top of the chocolate to add a little extra elegance to this popcorn before packaging it and giving it away.

8 cups popped popcorn (see page 7)
1 cup white chocolate or vanilla melting candy (see page 11)
3 teaspoons pistachio-flavored instant pudding mix (see Note)
½ cup chopped pistachios
¼ cup milk chocolate melting candy (see page 9)

Pour the popcorn into a large bowl and remove any unpopped kernels.

Place the white melting candy in a medium microwave-safe bowl. Microwave on medium power for 1 minute. Stir until melted and smooth. If needed, add additional heating time in 30-second increments, stirring after each time, until the candy is melted and smooth. Whisk the pudding mix into the melting candy.

Pour the melted candy over the popcorn, but do not stir yet.

Add the pistachios to the popcorn bowl. Using a large rubber spatula, gently stir to coat.

Spread the popcorn mixture on a large piece of parchment paper or a large silicone baking mat.

Place the milk chocolate melting candy in a small microwave-safe bowl. Microwave on medium power for 30 seconds. Stir until melted and smooth. If needed, heat for an additional 30 seconds.

Transfer the chocolate to a zip-top bag or piping bag. Press all the air out of the bag and snip the corner off. Use this bag to drizzle the chocolate across the popcorn.

Allow to cool until the candy coating has hardened, about 20 minutes. Break into pieces before packaging or transferring to a bowl to serve immediately. The popcorn may be stored in an airtight container for up to 4 days.

NOTE: The pudding mix will not change the color of the candy coating to a bright green. If you want the coating to be colored, use green-colored melting candy instead of white melting candy (see page 11).

Prep time: 10 minutes
Cook time: 0 minutes
Cool time: 20 minutes

cookies and cream popcorn

SERVES: 6

Is there a dynamic dessert duo more beloved than cookies and cream? They seem to make an appearance in nearly every dessert: breads, cupcakes, cookies, puddings, ice creams, cakes, frostings, and so many others. Why not popcorn? Crunchy, creamy, chocolate sandwich cookies are coated in white melting candy and drizzled with another layer of chocolate.

8 cups popped popcorn (see page 7)
1 cup white chocolate or vanilla melting candy (see page 11)
1 cup crumbled chocolate sandwich cookies
¼ cup milk chocolate melting candy (see page 9)

Pour the popcorn into a large bowl and remove any unpopped kernels.

Place the white melting candy in a medium microwave-safe bowl. Microwave on medium power for 1 minute. Stir until melted and smooth. If needed, add additional heating time in 30-second increments, stirring after each time, until the candy is melted and smooth.

Pour the melted candy over the popcorn, but do not stir yet.

Add the crumbled cookies to the popcorn bowl. Using a large rubber spatula, gently stir to coat.

Spread the popcorn mixture on a large piece of parchment paper or a large silicone baking mat.

Place the milk chocolate melting candy in a small microwave-safe bowl. Microwave on medium power for 30 seconds. Stir until melted and smooth. If needed, heat for an additional 30 seconds.

Transfer the chocolate to a zip-top bag or piping bag. Press all the air out of the bag and snip the corner off. Use this bag to drizzle the chocolate across the popcorn.

Allow to cool until the candy coating has hardened, about 20 minutes. Break into pieces before packaging or transferring to a bowl to serve immediately. The popcorn may be stored in an airtight container for up to 4 days.

Prep time: 10 minutes
Cook time: 0 minutes
Cool time: 20 minutes

pecan praline popcorn

SERVES: 6

Pecan pralines are traditionally a southern confection, made with a buttery toffee and southern-grown pecans. This recipe coats popcorn's nooks and crannies in that traditional rich and buttery toffee flavor, and then bakes the popcorn to a crisp. Don't be surprised if you're speaking with a sweet Georgia southern drawl after a bite or two!

8 cups popped popcorn (see page 7)
¾ cup packed light brown sugar
6 tablespoons (¾ stick) butter
3 tablespoons light corn syrup
½ teaspoon butter extract
¼ teaspoon baking soda
1 cup pecan halves

Preheat the oven to 300°F. Line a baking sheet with parchment paper or a silicone baking mat.

Pour the popcorn into a large bowl and remove any unpopped kernels.

In a medium saucepan over medium heat, stir together the brown sugar, butter, and corn syrup until the butter has melted and the mixture reaches a slow bubble. Stop stirring and allow the mixture to boil for 4 minutes.

Remove from the heat immediately and mix in the butter extract and baking soda (the baking soda will bubble up a bit). Stir in the pecan halves.

Pour the caramel-pecan mixture over the popcorn. Using a large rubber spatula, gently stir to coat.

Spread the popcorn evenly onto the prepared baking sheet.

Bake the popcorn for 10 to 15 minutes. A 10-minute bake will yield chewy popcorn, while a 15-minute bake will yield crunchy popcorn.

Let cool in the pan for about 10 minutes before transferring to a bowl and serving.

Serve chewy popcorn immediately. Crunchy popcorn may be stored in an airtight container for up to 1 week. Let cool completely before packaging.

Prep time: 10 minutes
Cook time: 10 to 15 minutes
Cool time: 10 minutes

gooey marshmallow popcorn

SERVES: 6

My mom would make this for us on family game nights. The gooey popcorn made our fingers sticky, which led to many sticky board games and card decks. But that was okay by us. We were willing to sacrifice a deck or two of cards in exchange for this marvelous popcorn.

8 cups popped popcorn (see page 7)
4 cups miniature marshmallows
3 tablespoons butter
1 cup plain milk chocolate candies, miniature size

Pour the popcorn into a large bowl and remove any unpopped kernels.

Place the marshmallows and butter in a large microwave-safe bowl. Microwave on medium power for 1 minute. Stir until the marshmallows are melted and smooth. If needed, add additional heating time in 30-second increments, stirring after each time.

Use a sturdy rubber spatula to scrape the melted marshmallow into the popcorn bowl. Add the chocolate candies and gently stir to coat. Serve immediately. The popcorn may be stored in an airtight container for up to 1 day.

Prep time: 10 minutes
Cook time: 0 minutes
Cool time: 0 minutes

lemon-lime popcorn

SERVES: 6

Lemon-lime soda was one of my favorite childhood treats, and I enjoyed creating a popcorn recipe using lemon and lime flavors. This recipe is a lot of fun visually as well if you use colored melting candy. Use yellow melting candy for the lemon half and green melting candy for the lime half. After the coatings have set, mix them together so the popcorn looks as great as it tastes.

> 8 cups popped popcorn (see page 7)
> 1 cup white chocolate or vanilla melting candy (see page 11), divided
> 1 tablespoon lime-flavored instant gelatin mix
> 1 tablespoon lemon-flavored instant gelatin mix (see Note)

Divide the popcorn evenly into two large bowls and remove any unpopped kernels.

Place ½ cup of the white melting candy in a medium microwave-safe bowl. Microwave on medium power for 30 seconds. Stir until melted and smooth. If needed, add additional heating time in 30-second increments, stirring after each time, until the candy is melted and smooth. Whisk the lime-flavored gelatin mix into the melting candy.

Pour the melted candy over one bowl of popcorn. Using a large spatula, gently stir to coat.

Spread the popcorn mixture on a large piece of parchment paper or a large silicone baking mat. Allow to cool until the chocolate coating has hardened, about 20 minutes.

While the first batch of popcorn is cooling, place the remaining ½ cup white melting candy in a medium microwave-safe bowl. Microwave on medium power for 30 seconds. Stir until melted and smooth. If needed, add additional heating time in 30-second increments, stirring after each time, until the candy is melted and smooth. Whisk the lemon-flavored gelatin mix into the melting candy.

Pour the melted candy over the remaining bowl of popcorn. Using a large spatula, gently stir to coat.

Spread the popcorn mixture on a large piece of parchment paper or a large silicone baking mat. Allow to cool until the candy coating has hardened, about 20 minutes.

Once both batches of popcorn are cooled enough that the candy coats are set, mix them together in one bowl and serve immediately. The popcorn may be stored in an airtight container for up to 4 days.

NOTE: The gelatin mix will not change the color of the candy coating to a bright green or yellow. If you want the coating to be colored, use green- and yellow-colored melting candy instead of white melting candy (see page 11).

Prep time: 15 minutes
Cook time: 0 minutes
Cool time: 20 minutes

classic kettle corn

SERVES: 8

Kettle corn is a staple at street fairs and carnivals nationwide. And for good reason. Its aroma carries easily through a crowd, drawing people to watch the sugar-coated popcorn pop in large steaming kettles. It's almost as much fun to watch pop as it is to eat—almost! This recipe includes a bit of cinnamon to make this treat extra-tasty.

¼ **cup vegetable or canola oil**
½ **cup popcorn kernels**
½ **cup granulated sugar**
1 **teaspoon ground cinnamon**
3 **tablespoons butter, melted**

Pour the oil into a large, deep pot with a lid. Heat the oil over medium-high heat. Place one popcorn kernel in the pot with the oil.

When the test kernel pops, the oil has reached the correct temperature. Mix the sugar and cinnamon into the oil.

Add the popcorn kernels and cover. Shake the pot back and forth over the heat. The kernels should start popping within 2 or 3 minutes.

Once the popping has stopped, remove the pot from the heat immediately (see Note).

Spread the popcorn on a large piece of parchment paper or a large silicone baking mat to let the popcorn cool slightly and allow the sugar to harden.

While the popcorn is cooling, drizzle the butter over the top. Serve immediately. The popcorn may be stored in an airtight container for up to 4 days.

NOTE: Do not attempt to cook the popcorn until it is brown, or it will burn. The popcorn will continue to cook for a bit after it is removed from the heat and may turn slightly golden.

Prep time: 5 minutes
Cook time: 15 minutes
Cool time: 5 minutes

browned butter popcorn

SERVES: 4 TO 6

Browning butter can be a tricky business, but learning how to do this correctly will yield dividends in taste. The trick to browning butter is simple: Never take your eyes off the butter. If you don't burn the butter, you'll end up with a rich, nutty flavor that adds extra depth and substance to any other flavor it is combined with. I like browned butter best in sweet pairings, so this recipe calls for sugar. But if you're feeling adventurous, try using browned butter in place of the melted butter in some of the savory recipes in this book.

8 cups popped popcorn (see page 7)
5 tablespoons butter
1 tablespoon granulated sugar
½ teaspoon salt

Pour the popcorn into a large bowl and remove any unpopped kernels.

Place the butter in a medium saucepan over medium-high heat and stir continuously until melted. Continue stirring for an additional 4 to 5 minutes, until little brown bits begin to form at the bottom of the pan and the butter changes to a golden brown color.

Remove the saucepan from the heat immediately and continue to stir for another minute.

Pour the browned butter over the popcorn. Sprinkle the sugar and salt over the popcorn and gently toss to coat. Serve immediately.

Prep time: 5 minutes
Cook time: 10 minutes
Cool time: 0 minutes

bear claw popcorn

SERVES: 6

Bear Claw is one of my favorite ice cream flavors, and I thought it would be absolutely perfect in popcorn. All the same ingredients are here: chocolate, caramel-filled chocolate candy cups, and cashews. If you're a chocolate lover of any sort, this popcorn is bound to be right up your alley.

8 cups popped popcorn (see page 7)
¾ cup milk chocolate melting candy (see page 9)
½ cup caramel-filled chocolate candy cups
½ cup chopped cashews

Pour the popcorn into a large bowl and remove any unpopped kernels.

Place the chocolate melting candy in a medium microwave-safe bowl. Microwave on medium power for 1 minute. Stir until melted and smooth. If needed, add additional heating time in 30-second increments, stirring after each time, until the candy is melted and smooth.

Pour the melted candy over the popcorn, but do not stir yet.

Add the caramel-filled cups and cashews to the popcorn bowl. Using a large rubber spatula, gently stir to coat.

Spread the popcorn mixture on a large piece of parchment paper or a large silicone baking mat.

Allow to cool until the chocolate coating has hardened, about 20 minutes. Break into pieces before packaging or transferring to a bowl to serve immediately. The popcorn may be stored in an airtight container for up to 4 days.

Prep time: 10 minutes
Cook time: 0 minutes
Cool time: 20 minutes

white chocolate snickerdoodle popcorn

SERVES: 6

The most popular recipe on my blog, by far, is for White Chocolate Snickerdoodle Cookies. Folks just can't get enough of them (myself included). It's no wonder why: White chocolate and cinnamon belong together, utterly and completely. They also come together perfectly in this popcorn. White chocolate coats the popcorn and bits of cinnamon crumble to make it taste like you are actually eating bites of snickerdoodles along with the popcorn.

8 cups popped popcorn (see page 7)
¾ cup all-purpose flour
3 tablespoons packed light brown sugar
2 teaspoon ground cinnamon
½ cup (1 stick) butter, cold and cubed
1 cup white chocolate or vanilla melting candy (see page 11)
3 tablespoons granulated sugar

Pour the popcorn into a large bowl and remove any unpopped kernels.

Use a fork or food processor to mix the flour, brown sugar, 1 teaspoon of the cinnamon, and butter until a crumble mixture forms.

Add the crumble mixture to the popcorn bowl.

Place the white melting candy in a medium microwave-safe bowl. Microwave on medium power for 1 minute. Stir until melted and smooth. If needed, add additional heating time in 30-second increments, stirring after each time, until the candy is melted and smooth.

Pour the melted candy over the popcorn. Using a large rubber spatula, gently stir to coat.

Spread the popcorn mixture on a large piece of parchment paper or a large silicone baking mat.

In a small bowl, mix together the granulated sugar and remaining cinnamon. Sprinkle the cinnamon sugar over the popcorn mixture.

Allow to cool until the candy coating has hardened, about 20 minutes. Break into pieces before packaging or transferring to a bowl to serve immediately. The popcorn may be stored in an airtight container for up to 4 days.

Prep time: 15 minutes
Cook time: 0 minutes
Cool time: 20 minutes

chocolate-covered pretzel popcorn

SERVES: 6

This recipe is super-simple and super-delicious. Just take two favorite snack foods and cover them in chocolate for a sweet and salty mix everyone will love.

8 cups popped popcorn (see page 7)
¾ cup milk chocolate melting candy (see page 9)
½ cup mini pretzel twists
1 teaspoon coarse sea salt

Pour the popcorn into a large bowl and remove any unpopped kernels.

Place the chocolate melting candy in a medium microwave-safe bowl. Microwave on medium power for 1 minute. Stir until melted and smooth. If needed, add additional heating time in 30-second increments, stirring after each time, until the candy is melted and smooth.

Pour the melted candy over the popcorn, but do not stir yet.

Add the pretzels to the popcorn bowl. Using a large rubber spatula, gently stir to coat.

Spread the popcorn mixture on a large piece of parchment paper or a large silicone baking mat. Sprinkle the sea salt over the popcorn.

Allow to cool until the chocolate coating has hardened, about 20 minutes. Break into pieces before packaging or transferring to a bowl to serve immediately. The popcorn may be stored in an airtight container for up to 4 days.

Prep time: 10 minutes
Cook time: 0 minutes
Cool time: 20 minutes

neapolitan popcorn

SERVES: 6

This popcorn recipe is triple the fun. Vanilla, strawberry, and chocolate come together in this popcorn mix to create a great spin on one of everybody's favorite ice cream flavors. Which flavor is your favorite?

9 cups popped popcorn (see page 7)
1 cup white chocolate or vanilla melting candy (see page 11), divided
1 tablespoon strawberry-flavored instant gelatin mix
½ cup milk chocolate melting candy (see page 9)

Divide the popcorn evenly into three large bowls and remove any unpopped kernels.

Place ½ cup of the white melting candy in a medium microwave-safe bowl. Microwave on medium power for 30 seconds. Stir until melted and smooth. If needed, add additional heating time in 30-second increments, stirring after each time, until the candy is melted and smooth. Whisk the strawberry-flavored gelatin mix into the melting candy.

Pour the melted candy over one bowl of popcorn. Using a large spatula, gently stir to coat.

Spread the popcorn mixture on a large piece of parchment paper or a large silicone baking mat. Allow to cool until the candy coating has hardened, about 20 minutes.

While the first batch of popcorn is cooling, place the remaining ½ cup white melting candy in a medium microwave-safe bowl. Microwave on medium power for 30 seconds. Stir until melted and smooth. If needed, add additional heating time in 30-second increments, stirring after each time, until the candy is melted and smooth.

Pour the melted candy over one bowl of popcorn. Using a large spatula, gently stir to coat.

Spread the popcorn mixture on a large piece of parchment paper or a large silicone baking mat. Allow to cool until the candy coating has hardened, about 20 minutes.

While the first two batches of popcorn are cooling, place the milk chocolate melting candy in a medium microwave-safe bowl. Microwave on medium power for 30 seconds. Stir until melted and smooth. If needed, add additional heating time in 30-second increments, stirring after each time, until the candy is melted and smooth.

Pour the melted candy over the remaining bowl of popcorn. Using a large rubber spatula, gently stir to coat.

Spread the popcorn mixture on a large piece of parchment paper or

a large silicone baking mat. Allow to cool until the candy coating has hardened, about 20 minutes.

Once all batches of popcorn are cooled enough that the candy coats are set, mix them together in one bowl and serve immediately. The popcorn may be stored in an airtight container for up to 4 days.

Prep time: 20 minutes
Cook time: 0 minutes
Cool time: 20 minutes

heavenly hash popcorn

SERVES: 6

I worked in the university bookstore when I was in college, and it was well known for its wide variety of homemade fudge flavors. Among my very favorites was heavenly hash, which inspired this popcorn recipe. The gooey marshmallow topped with chocolate and almonds, all coating the popcorn, make this a decadent treat you won't want to stop eating.

8 cups popped popcorn (see page 7)
4 cups miniature marshmallows
3 tablespoons butter
¾ cup milk chocolate melting candy (see page 9)
½ cup chopped almonds

Pour the popcorn into a large bowl and remove any unpopped kernels.

Place the marshmallows and butter in a large microwave-safe bowl. Microwave on medium power for 1 minute. Stir until the marshmallows are melted and smooth. If needed, add additional heating time in 30-second increments, stirring after each time.

Use a sturdy rubber spatula to scrape the melted marshmallow into the popcorn bowl and gently stir to coat.

Place the chocolate melting candy in a medium microwave-safe bowl. Microwave on medium power for 30 seconds. Stir until melted and smooth. If needed, add additional heating time in 30-second increments, stirring after each time, until the candy is melted and smooth.

Pour the melted candy over the popcorn. Using a large rubber spatula, gently stir to coat.

Spread the popcorn mixture on a large piece of parchment paper or a large silicone baking mat. Sprinkle the almonds over the popcorn.

Allow to cool until the chocolate coating has hardened, about 20 minutes. Break into pieces before packaging or transferring to a bowl to serve immediately. The popcorn may be stored in an airtight container for up to 2 days.

Prep time: 15 minutes
Cook time: 0 minutes
Cool time: 20 minutes

salted toffee chocolate popcorn

SERVES: 6

This popcorn is the perfect blend of salty and sweet and has a little extra crunch thanks to the toffee bits. It is simple and delicious, and perfect for packaging in pretty bags with ribbons for friends.

8 cups popped popcorn (see page 7)
1 cup milk chocolate melting candy (see page 9)
1 cup chocolate-covered toffee bits, divided
1 tablespoon coarse sea salt, divided

Pour the popcorn into a large bowl and remove any unpopped kernels.

Place the chocolate melting candy in a medium microwave-safe bowl. Microwave on medium power for 1 minute. Stir until melted and smooth. If needed, add additional heating time in 30-second increments, stirring after each time, until the candy is melted and smooth.

Pour the melted candy over the popcorn, but do not stir yet.

Add ¾ cup of the chocolate-covered toffee bits and 1½ teaspoons of the sea salt to the popcorn bowl. Using a large rubber spatula, gently stir to coat.

Spread the popcorn mixture on a large piece of parchment paper or a large silicone baking mat. Sprinkle the remaining ¼ cup chocolate-covered toffee bits and 1½ teaspoons sea salt over the popcorn.

Allow to cool until the chocolate coating has hardened, about 20 minutes. Break into pieces before packaging or transferring to a bowl to serve immediately. The popcorn may be stored in an airtight container for up to 4 days.

Prep time: 10 minutes
Cook time: 0 minutes
Cool time: 20 minutes

death by chocolate popcorn

SERVES: 6

If you have to go, death by chocolate is the way to do it.
This recipe is loaded to the brim with chocolate cookies,
candies, brownies, chocolate chips, and a decadent dark
chocolate drizzle. This one is for ultimate chocolate lovers
everywhere.

8 cups popped popcorn (see page 7)
1 cup milk chocolate melting candy (see page 9)
½ cup crumbled chocolate sandwich cookies
½ cup plain milk chocolate candies, miniature size
½ cup crumbled brownies (see page 70)
¼ cup dark chocolate melting candy (see page 9)
½ cup mini chocolate chips

Pour the popcorn into a large bowl and remove any unpopped kernels.

Place the milk chocolate melting candy in a medium microwave-safe
bowl. Microwave on medium power for 1 minute. Stir until melted and
smooth. If needed, add additional heating time in 30-second increments,
stirring after each time, until the candy is melted and smooth.

Pour the melted candy over the popcorn, but do not stir yet.

Add the sandwich cookies, plain milk chocolate candies, and brownies to
the popcorn bowl. Using a large rubber spatula, gently stir to coat.

Spread the popcorn mixture on a large piece of parchment paper or a
large silicone baking mat.

Place the dark chocolate melting candy in a small microwave-safe
bowl. Microwave on medium power for 30 seconds. Stir until melted and
smooth. If needed, heat for an additional 30 seconds.

Transfer the dark chocolate to a zip-top bag or piping bag. Press all
the air out of the bag and snip the corner off. Use this bag to drizzle
the chocolate across the popcorn. Sprinkle the chocolate chips over the
popcorn.

Allow to cool until the chocolate coating has hardened, about 20
minutes. Break into pieces before packaging or transferring to a bowl to
serve immediately. The popcorn may be stored in an airtight container for
up to 4 days.

Prep time: 10 minutes
Cook time: 0 minutes
Cool time: 20 minutes

chunky monkey popcorn

SERVES: 6

This popcorn reinvents a classic ice cream flavor. Banana
pudding mix gives this popcorn a unique and delicious
flavor, while the walnuts and banana chips give it a
satisfying crunch. A chocolate coating seals the deal and
makes this fun recipe a winner.

8 cups popped popcorn (see page 7)
1 cup milk chocolate melting candy (see page 9)
1 tablespoon banana-flavored instant pudding mix
½ cup dried banana chips
½ cup chopped walnuts

Pour the popcorn into a large bowl and remove any unpopped kernels.

Place the chocolate melting candy in a medium microwave-safe bowl.
Microwave on medium power for 1 minute. Stir until melted and smooth.
If needed, add additional heating time in 30-second increments, stirring
after each time, until the candy is melted and smooth. Whisk the pudding
mix into the melting candy.

Pour the melted candy over the popcorn, but do not stir yet.

Add the banana chips and walnuts to the popcorn bowl. Using a large
rubber spatula, gently stir to coat.

Spread the popcorn mixture on a large piece of parchment paper or a
large silicone baking mat.

Allow to cool until the chocolate coating has hardened, about 20
minutes. Break into pieces before packaging or transferring to a bowl to
serve immediately. The popcorn may be stored in an airtight container for
up to 4 days.

Prep time: 10 minutes
Cook time: 0 minutes
Cool time: 20 minutes

popcorn fun for kids

peanut butter fluff popcorn

SERVES: 6

A Fluffernutter sandwich is made by spreading peanut butter and marshmallow crème between two slices of bread. It is considered the ultimate sandwich by many a lunchbox-toting kid. In celebration of those flavors, I'm pairing peanut butter with marshmallows in this delicious popcorn recipe.

> 8 cups popped popcorn (see page 7)
> 1 cup miniature marshmallows
> 2 cups white chocolate or vanilla melting candy (see page 11)
> ¼ cup peanut butter

Pour the popcorn into a large bowl and remove any unpopped kernels. Add the marshmallows to the popcorn.

Place the white melting candy and peanut butter in a medium microwave-safe bowl. Microwave on medium power for 1 minute. Stir until melted and smooth. If needed, add additional heating time in 30-second increments, stirring after each time, until the candy is melted and smooth.

Pour the melted candy over the popcorn. Using a large rubber spatula, gently stir to coat.

Spread the popcorn mixture on a large piece of parchment paper or a large silicone baking mat.

Allow to cool until the candy coating has hardened, about 20 minutes. Break into pieces before packaging or transferring to a bowl to serve immediately. The popcorn may be stored in an airtight container for up to 4 days.

Prep time: 10 minutes
Cook time: 0 minutes
Cool time: 20 minutes

gooey s'mores popcorn

SERVES: 6

As a kid, I thought s'mores were the best thing about summer. As an adult, I still think s'mores are the best part of the season. Now you can enjoy these classic summertime and childhood favorite flavors year-round. Gooey marshmallow coats graham crackers, chocolate bar pieces, and popcorn, creating the ultimate s'mores popcorn experience.

8 cups popped popcorn (see page 7)
4 cups miniature marshmallows
3 tablespoons butter
½ cup chopped milk chocolate candy bars
½ cup crumbled graham crackers

Pour the popcorn into a large bowl and remove any unpopped kernels.

Place the marshmallows and butter in a large microwave-safe bowl. Microwave on medium power for 1 minute. Stir until the marshmallows are melted and smooth. If needed, add additional heating time in 30-second increments, stirring after each time.

Use a sturdy rubber spatula to scrape the melted marshmallow into the popcorn bowl. Add the candy bar pieces and graham cracker pieces and gently stir to coat. Serve immediately. The popcorn may be stored in an airtight container for up to 2 days.

Prep time: 10 minutes
Cook time: 0 minutes
Cool time: 0 minutes

ocean-blue popcorn with fish

SERVES: 6

This popcorn is a classic kid favorite. It's crunchy and sweet, and it's blue and full of fish. What's not to love?

10 cups popped popcorn (see page 7)
4 tablespoons (½ stick) butter
3 tablespoons light corn syrup
½ cup granulated sugar
One 3-ounce package blue-colored instant gelatin mix
½ cup gummy-style candy fish

Pour the popcorn into a large bowl and remove any unpopped kernels.

In a medium saucepan over medium heat, stir the butter and corn syrup until the butter has melted. Add the sugar and gelatin mix and whisk until dissolved.

Increase the heat to medium and stir continuously until the mixture reaches a slow bubble. Stop stirring and allow the mixture to boil for 2 to 3 minutes. If the mixture boils too long, it will turn green.

Pour the blue mixture over the popcorn. Using a large rubber spatula, gently stir to coat. Add the candy fish to the popcorn and stir to coat.

Spread the popcorn mixture on a large piece of parchment paper or a large silicone baking mat. Keep little hands away from the popcorn until it has completely cooled. The sugar mixture is extremely hot and sticks to skin on contact.

Allow to cool until the coating has hardened, about 20 minutes. Break into pieces before packaging or transferring to a bowl to serve immediately. The popcorn may be stored in an airtight container for up to 1 week.

Prep time: 15 minutes
Cook time: 15 minutes
Cool time: 20 minutes

berry puffs cereal popcorn

SERVES: 6

I love kids' cereal. It's colorful and sweet and fun. In this recipe the crunchy sweetness of the cereal combines perfectly with the subtle flavors of the popcorn. Once they're tossed together in a white candy coating, you'll find yourself unable to stop with just one handful.

8 cups popped popcorn (see page 7)
1 cup white chocolate or vanilla melting candy (see page 11)
1 cup berry-flavored puffs cereal

Pour the popcorn into a large bowl and remove any unpopped kernels.

Place the white melting candy in a medium microwave-safe bowl. Microwave on medium power for 1 minute. Stir until melted and smooth. If needed, add additional heating time in 30-second increments, stirring after each time, until the candy is melted and smooth.

Pour the melted candy over the popcorn. Add the puffs cereal to the bowl. Using a large rubber spatula, gently stir to coat.

Spread the popcorn mixture on a large piece of parchment paper or a large silicone baking mat.

Allow to cool until the candy coating has hardened, about 20 minutes. Break into pieces before packaging or transferring to a bowl to serve immediately. The popcorn may be stored in an airtight container for up to 4 days.

Prep time: 10 minutes
Cook time: 0 minutes
Cool time: 20 minutes

animal cracker popcorn

SERVES: 6

This recipe brings the classic look and taste of colorful, candy-coated animal crackers to popcorn. Pink-sprinkled animal crackers were a favorite of mine as a kid. Sprinkles make food special and every kid in the world knows it. Make your kids feel extra-special by letting them help you whip up this fun and colorful popcorn treat.

8 cups popped popcorn (see page 7)
1 cup pink melting candy (see page 11)
¼ cup rainbow-colored nonpareils

Pour the popcorn into a large bowl and remove any unpopped kernels.

Place the pink melting candy in a medium microwave-safe bowl. Microwave on medium power for 1 minute. Stir until melted and smooth. If needed, add additional heating time in 30-second increments, stirring after each time, until the candy is melted and smooth.

Pour the melted candy over the popcorn. Using a large rubber spatula, gently stir to coat. Sprinkle the nonpareils over the popcorn and gently toss to coat.

Spread the popcorn mixture on a large piece of parchment paper or a large silicone baking mat.

Allow to cool until the candy coating has hardened, about 20 minutes. Break into pieces before packaging or transferring to a bowl to serve immediately. The popcorn may be stored in an airtight container for up to 4 days.

Prep time: 15 minutes
Cook time: 0 minutes
Cool time: 20 minutes

strawberry fizz popcorn

SERVES: 6

Pop Rocks give this popcorn a major fun factor. Enjoy
the sweet strawberry taste and get ready to smile as this
popcorn fizzes and pops in your mouth.

10 cups popped popcorn (see page 7)
4 tablespoons (½ stick) butter
3 tablespoons light corn syrup
½ cup granulated sugar
One 3-ounce package red-colored instant gelatin mix
¼ cup strawberry-flavored Pop Rocks

Pour the popcorn into a large bowl and remove any unpopped kernels.

In a medium saucepan over medium heat, stir the butter and corn syrup
until the butter has melted. Add the sugar and gelatin mix and whisk until
dissolved.

Increase the heat to medium and stir continuously until the mixture
reaches a slow bubble. Stop stirring and allow the mixture to boil for 5
minutes.

Pour the red mixture over the popcorn. Using a large rubber spatula,
gently stir to coat. Add the Pop Rocks and stir to coat.

Spread the popcorn mixture on a large piece of parchment paper or a
large silicone baking mat. Keep little hands away from the popcorn until
it has completely cooled. The sugar mixture is extremely hot and sticks to
skin on contact.

Allow to cool until the coating has hardened, about 20 minutes. Break
into pieces before packaging or transferring to a bowl to serve immediately.
The popcorn may be stored in an airtight container for up to 1 week.

Prep time: 15 minutes
Cook time: 15 minutes
Cool time: 20 minutes

holiday and seasonal

chocolate-covered strawberry popcorn

SERVES: 6

Chocolate-covered strawberries are an iconic way to say "I love you" on Valentine's Day. This year, say it with chocolate-covered strawberry popcorn. This popcorn packages beautifully and makes a sweet gift for all the special people in your life.

8 cups popped popcorn (see page 7)
1 cup white chocolate or vanilla melting candy (see page 11)
1 tablespoon strawberry-flavored instant gelatin mix
¼ cup milk chocolate melting candy (see page 9)

Pour the popcorn into a large bowl and remove any unpopped kernels.

Place the white melting candy in a medium microwave-safe bowl. Microwave on medium power for 1 minute. Stir until melted and smooth. If needed, add additional heating time in 30-second increments, stirring after each time, until the candy is melted and smooth. Whisk the gelatin mix into the melting candy.

Pour the melted candy over the popcorn. Using a large spatula, gently stir to coat.

Spread the popcorn mixture on a large piece of parchment paper or a large silicone baking mat.

Place the milk chocolate melting candy in a small microwave-safe bowl. Microwave on medium power for 30 seconds. Stir until melted and smooth. If needed, heat for an additional 30 seconds.

Transfer the chocolate to a zip-top bag or piping bag. Press all the air out of the bag and snip the corner off. Use this bag to drizzle the chocolate across the popcorn.

Allow to cool until the candy coating has hardened, about 20 minutes. Break into pieces before packaging or transferring to a bowl to serve immediately. The popcorn may be stored in an airtight container for up to 4 days.

Prep time: 10 minutes
Cook time: 0 minutes
Cool time: 20 minutes

piña colada popcorn

SERVES: 6

Pineapple- and coconut-flavored candy coatings and sweet coconut invite the islands right into your kitchen.

> 8 cups popped popcorn (see page 7)
> 1 cup white chocolate or vanilla melting candy (see page 11), divided
> 1 tablespoon pineapple-flavored instant gelatin mix (see Note)
> 1 tablespoon coconut cream–flavored instant pudding mix
> ½ cup sweetened flaked coconut

Divide the popcorn evenly into two large bowls and remove any unpopped kernels.

Place ½ cup of the white melting candy in a medium microwave-safe bowl. Microwave on medium power for 30 seconds. Stir until melted and smooth. If needed, add additional heating time in 30-second increments, stirring after each time, until the candy is melted and smooth. Whisk the pineapple-flavored gelatin mix into the melting candy.

Pour the melted candy over one bowl of popcorn. Using a large spatula, gently stir to coat.

Spread the popcorn mixture on a large piece of parchment paper or a large silicone baking mat. Allow to cool until the candy coating has hardened, about 20 minutes.

While the first batch of popcorn is cooling, place the remaining ½ cup white melting candy in a medium microwave-safe bowl. Microwave on medium power for 30 seconds. Stir until melted and smooth. If needed, add additional heating time in 30-second increments, stirring after each time, until the candy is melted and smooth. Whisk the coconut cream–flavored pudding mix into the melting candy.

Pour the melted candy over the remaining bowl of popcorn. Add the coconut. Using a large spatula, gently stir to coat.

Spread the popcorn mixture on a large piece of parchment paper or a large silicone baking mat. Allow to cool until the candy coating has hardened, about 20 minutes.

Once both batches of popcorn are cooled enough that the candy coats are set, mix them together in one bowl to serve immediately. The popcorn may be stored in an airtight container for up to 4 days.

NOTE: The gelatin mix will not change the color of the candy coating (see page 11).

Prep time: 15 minutes
Cook time: 0 minutes
Cool time: 20 minutes

root beer float popcorn

SERVES: 6

Nothing says summer quite like a root beer float. If you thought popcorn couldn't taste like a root beer float, you're in for a surprising treat. The crispy popcorn complements the classic flavor of a float perfectly and creates a fun summertime snack.

8 cups popped popcorn (see page 7)
1 cup white chocolate or vanilla melting candy (see page 11)
1 tablespoon sweetened condensed milk (see Note)
2 tablespoons root beer extract

Pour the popcorn into a large bowl and remove any unpopped kernels.

Place the white melting candy in a medium microwave-safe bowl. Microwave on medium power for 1 minute. Stir until melted and smooth. If needed, add additional heating time in 30-second increments, stirring after each time, until the candy is melted and smooth.

Whisk together the condensed milk and root beer extract in a small bowl. Pour the root beer mixture into the white melting candy and mix well.

Pour the melted candy over the popcorn. Using a large rubber spatula, gently stir to coat.

Spread the popcorn mixture on a large piece of parchment paper or a large silicone baking mat.

Allow to cool for 20 minutes and serve immediately. The popcorn may be stored in an airtight container for up to 2 days.

NOTE: The addition of the sweetened condensed milk allows the root beer extract to be mixed into the popcorn without causing the candy coating to seize. However, it keeps the candy coating from setting up and hardening completely.

Prep time: 10 minutes
Cook time: 0 minutes
Cool time: 20 minutes

firecracker popcorn

SERVES: 6

This popcorn is bursting with colors, flavors, and textures that are just perfect for your Fourth of July celebrations. Pop Rocks add red and blue colors and a literal explosion in your mouth.

8 cups popped popcorn (see page 7)
¾ cup white chocolate or vanilla melting candy (see page 11)
2 tablespoons red Pop Rocks
2 tablespoons blue Pop Rocks

Pour the popcorn into a large bowl and remove any unpopped kernels.

Place the white melting candy in a medium microwave-safe bowl. Microwave on medium power for 1 minute. Stir until melted and smooth. If needed, add additional heating time in 30-second increments, stirring after each time, until the candy is melted and smooth.

Pour the melted candy over the popcorn. Using a large rubber spatula, gently stir to coat.

Spread the popcorn mixture on a large piece of parchment paper or a large silicone baking mat. Sprinkle both the red and blue Pop Rocks over the popcorn.

Allow to cool until the candy coating has hardened, about 20 minutes. Break into pieces before packaging or transferring to a bowl to serve immediately. The popcorn may be stored in an airtight container for up to 4 days.

Prep time: 10 minutes
Cook time: 0 minutes
Cool time: 20 minutes

peanut brittle popcorn

SERVES: 6

The flavor and crunch of peanut brittle make for a perfect popcorn treat. Package this popcorn in small treat bags and hand them out to neighbors and friends to welcome in the rich flavors of autumn.

8 cups popped popcorn (see page 7)
½ cup granulated sugar
¼ cup light corn syrup
½ cup salted peanuts
½ teaspoon butter
½ teaspoon vanilla extract
½ teaspoon baking soda

Pour the popcorn into a large bowl and remove any unpopped kernels.

Mix the sugar and corn syrup in a medium microwave-safe bowl. Microwave the mixture on high power for 4 minutes. Mix in the salted peanuts and microwave for another 4 minutes. Stir in the butter and vanilla extract and microwave for another 2 minutes.

Stir in the baking soda (it will bubble up a bit).

Pour the peanut mixture over the popcorn. Using a large rubber spatula, stir gently to coat.

Spread the popcorn mixture on a large piece of parchment paper or a large silicone baking mat.

Allow to cool until the coating has hardened, about 20 minutes. Break into pieces before packaging or transferring to a bowl to serve immediately. The popcorn may be stored in an airtight container for up to 1 week.

Prep time: 5 minutes
Cook time: 10 minutes
Cool time: 20 minutes

pumpkin pie popcorn

SERVES: 6

Thanksgiving just isn't quite right without a great, big pumpkin pie on the table. Get ready for the ultimate pumpkin pie holiday by making this popcorn recipe. It's a fun twist on a classic holiday dessert.

8 cups popped popcorn (see page 7)
¾ cup crushed graham crackers
1 tablespoon granulated sugar
1 teaspoon ground cinnamon
3 tablespoons butter, melted
¾ cups white chocolate or vanilla melting candy (see page 11)
2 tablespoons canned pumpkin puree
½ teaspoon pumpkin pie spice

Pour the popcorn into a large bowl and remove any unpopped kernels.

Use a fork or food processor to mix the crushed graham crackers, sugar, cinnamon, and butter until a crumble mixture forms.

Place the white melting candy in a medium microwave-safe bowl. Microwave on medium power for 1 minute. Stir until melted and smooth. If needed, add additional heating time in 30-second increments, stirring after each time, until the candy is melted and smooth. Whisk the pumpkin puree and pumpkin pie spice into the melting candy.

Add the graham cracker mixture to the popcorn bowl. Pour the melted candy over the popcorn. Using a large rubber spatula, gently stir to coat.

Spread the popcorn mixture on a large piece of parchment paper or a large silicone baking mat.

Allow to cool until the candy coating has hardened, about 20 minutes. Break into pieces before packaging or transferring to a bowl to serve immediately. The popcorn may be stored in an airtight container for up to 2 days.

Prep time: 10 minutes
Cook time: 0 minutes
Cool time: 20 minutes

caramel pumpkin crunch popcorn

SERVES: 6

Enjoy some of the favorite flavors of fall in this crunchy and delicious popcorn recipe. Pumpkin and caramel combine beautifully to create an aromatic treat that will have you wanting to cozy up with someone you love (and a big bowl of popcorn).

8 cups popped popcorn (see page 7)
¾ cup packed light brown sugar
6 tablespoons canned pumpkin puree
3 tablespoons light corn syrup
½ teaspoon vanilla extract
½ teaspoon pumpkin pie spice
¼ teaspoon baking soda

Preheat the oven to 300°F. Line a baking sheet with parchment paper or a silicone baking mat.

Pour the popcorn into a large bowl and remove any unpopped kernels.

In a medium saucepan over medium heat, stir together the brown sugar, pumpkin puree, and corn syrup until the mixture reaches a slow bubble. Stop stirring and allow the mixture to boil for 4 minutes.

Remove from the heat immediately and mix in the vanilla extract, pumpkin pie spice, and baking soda (the baking soda will bubble up a bit).

Pour the pumpkin-caramel mixture over the popcorn. Using a large rubber spatula, gently stir to coat.

Spread the popcorn evenly onto the prepared baking sheet.

Bake the popcorn for 10 to 15 minutes. A 10-minute bake will yield chewy popcorn, while a 15-minute bake will yield crunchy popcorn.

Let cool in the pan for about 10 minutes before transferring to a bowl and serving.

Serve chewy popcorn immediately. Crunchy popcorn may be stored in an airtight container for up to 4 days. Let cool completely before packaging.

Prep time: 10 minutes
Cook time: 10 to 15 minutes
Cool time: 10 minutes

apple cider caramel popcorn

SERVES: 6

Put on your fuzziest socks, curl up in your coziest blanket, and dig into a great big bowl of this Apple Cider Caramel Popcorn. If you love the comforting flavors in the hot drink, this wintertime snack is sure to warm your heart (and tummy).

8 cups popped popcorn (see page 7)
¾ cup packed light brown sugar
6 tablespoons (¾ stick) butter
3 tablespoons light corn syrup
2 tablespoons apple cider–flavored instant drink mix (see Note)
½ teaspoon vanilla extract
¼ teaspoon baking soda

Preheat the oven to 300°F. Line a baking sheet with parchment paper or a silicone baking mat.

Pour the popcorn into a large bowl and remove any unpopped kernels.

In a medium saucepan over medium heat, stir together the brown sugar, butter, corn syrup, and apple cider mix until the butter has melted and the mixture reaches a slow bubble. Stop stirring and allow the mixture to boil for 4 minutes.

Remove from the heat immediately and mix in the vanilla extract and baking soda (the baking soda will bubble up a bit).

Pour the caramel-cider mixture over the popcorn. Using a large rubber spatula, gently stir to coat.

Spread the popcorn evenly onto the prepared baking sheet.

Bake the popcorn for 10 to 15 minutes. A 10-minute bake will yield chewy popcorn, while a 15-minute bake will yield crunchy popcorn.

Let cool in the pan for about 10 minutes before transferring to a bowl and serving.

Serve chewy popcorn immediately. Crunchy popcorn may be stored in an airtight container for up to 1 week. Let cool completely before packaging.

NOTE: This recipe calls for apple cider mix, which is a powder mixed into hot water to create a single serving of apple cider. It is often sold in small packages or envelopes and can be found next to the hot chocolate mixes in most grocery stores.

Prep time: 10 minutes
Cook time: 10 to 15 minutes
Cool time: 10 minutes

sweet potato pie popcorn

SERVES: 6

As a southern girl, I make sweet potato pie an integral part of my holiday festivities. It reminds me of my grandmother's kitchen and her countertops filled with delicious holiday foods. This popcorn delivers the classic flavors of sweet potato pie, but with less than half the time and effort. Plus, you don't have to wait for a big holiday dinner to dig into this treat.

8 cups popped popcorn (see page 7)
¾ cup all-purpose flour
3 tablespoons packed light brown sugar
1 teaspoon ground cinnamon
½ cup (1 stick) butter, cold and cubed
½ cup miniature marshmallows
¾ cup white chocolate or vanilla melting candy (see page 11)
1 tablespoon canned sweet potato pie filling

Pour the popcorn into a large bowl and remove any unpopped kernels.

Use a fork or food processor to mix the flour, brown sugar, cinnamon, and butter until a crumble mixture forms.

Add the crumble mixture and the marshmallows to the popcorn bowl.

Place the white melting candy in a medium microwave-safe bowl. Microwave on medium power for 1 minute. Stir until melted and smooth. If needed, add additional heating time in 30-second increments, stirring after each time, until the candy is melted and smooth. Whisk the sweet potato pie filling into the melting candy.

Pour the melted candy over the popcorn mixture. Using a large rubber spatula, gently stir to coat.

Spread the popcorn mixture on a large piece of parchment paper or a large silicone baking mat.

Allow to cool until the candy coating has hardened, about 20 minutes. Break into pieces before packaging or transferring to a bowl to serve immediately. The popcorn may be stored in an airtight container for up to 2 days.

Prep time: 10 minutes
Cook time: 0 minutes
Cool time: 20 minutes

hot chocolate popcorn

SERVES: 6

This popcorn recipe makes me want to pull out the ribbons and bows, tug on my mittens and earmuffs, and head out into the snow to sing carols and give my neighbors great big bags of these hot chocolaty munchies. Have a little extra fun with this popcorn and sprinkle peppermint bits on top.

> 8 cups popped popcorn (see page 7)
> ½ cup miniature marshmallows
> 1 cup milk chocolate melting candy (see page 9)
> 1 tablespoon instant hot chocolate mix
> ¼ cup white chocolate or vanilla melting candy (see page 11)

Pour the popcorn into a large bowl and remove any unpopped kernels. Add the marshmallows to the bowl.

Place the milk chocolate melting candy in a medium microwave-safe bowl. Microwave on medium power for 1 minute. Stir until melted and smooth. If needed, add additional heating time in 30-second increments, stirring after each time, until the candy is melted and smooth. Whisk the hot chocolate mix into the melting candy.

Pour the melted candy over the popcorn. Using a large rubber spatula, gently stir to coat.

Spread the popcorn mixture on a large piece of parchment paper or a large silicone baking mat.

Place the white melting candy in a small microwave-safe bowl. Microwave on medium power for 30 seconds. Stir until melted and smooth. If needed, heat for an additional 30 seconds.

Transfer the melted white candy to a zip-top bag or piping bag. Press all the air out of the bag and snip the corner off. Use this bag to drizzle the melted candy across the popcorn.

Allow to cool until the chocolate coating has hardened, about 20 minutes. Break into pieces before packaging or transferring to a bowl to serve immediately. The popcorn may be stored in an airtight container for up to 4 days.

Prep time: 10 minutes
Cook time: 0 minutes
Cool time: 20 minutes

chocolate peppermint bark popcorn

SERVES: 6

Chocolate and peppermint create an irresistible holiday flavor combination. Treat bags brimming with this popcorn would make beautiful and delicious gifts for family and friends.

8 cups popped popcorn (see page 7)
1 cup white chocolate or vanilla melting candy (see page 11)
½ cup crushed peppermint candy, divided
¼ cup milk chocolate melting candy (see page 9)

Pour the popcorn into a large bowl and remove any unpopped kernels.

Place the white melting candy in a medium microwave-safe bowl. Microwave on medium power for 1 minute. Stir until melted and smooth. If needed, add additional heating time in 30-second increments, stirring after each time, until the candy is melted and smooth. Mix ¼ cup of the crushed peppermint candy into the white melting candy.

Pour the melted candy over the popcorn. Using a large rubber spatula, gently stir to coat.

Spread the popcorn mixture on a large piece of parchment paper or a large silicone baking mat.

Place the milk chocolate melting candy in a small microwave-safe bowl. Microwave on medium power for 30 seconds. Stir until melted and smooth. If needed, heat for an additional 30 seconds.

Transfer the chocolate to a zip-top bag or piping bag. Press all the air out of the bag and snip the corner off. Use this bag to drizzle the chocolate across the popcorn. Sprinkle the remaining ¼ cup crushed peppermint candy over the popcorn.

Allow to cool until the candy coating has hardened, about 20 minutes. Break into pieces before packaging or transferring to a bowl to serve immediately. The popcorn may be stored in an airtight container for up to 4 days.

Prep time: 10 minutes
Cook time: 0 minutes
Cool time: 20 minutes

white chocolate cranberry cashew popcorn

SERVES: 6

This beautiful popcorn absolutely looks the part of a holiday treat. The white candy coating blankets the popcorn like a snowfall, and the bright peeps of red cranberries are reminiscent of the holiday red we decorate with. It's as delicious as it is beautiful, and if you can bear to share, your friends will be oh-so-impressed with this new holiday must-have treat.

8 cups popped popcorn (see page 7)
½ cup dried cranberries
½ cup cashew halves
1 cup white chocolate or vanilla melting candy (see page 11)

Pour the popcorn into a large bowl and remove any unpopped kernels. Add the dried cranberries and cashew halves to the bowl.

Place the white melting candy in a medium microwave-safe bowl. Microwave on medium power for 1 minute. Stir until melted and smooth. If needed, add additional heating time in 30-second increments, stirring after each time, until the candy is melted and smooth.

Pour the melted candy over the popcorn mixture. Using a large rubber spatula, gently stir to coat.

Spread the popcorn mixture on a large piece of parchment paper or a large silicone baking mat.

Allow to cool until the candy coating has hardened, about 20 minutes. Break into pieces before packaging or transferring to a bowl to serve immediately. The popcorn may be stored in an airtight container for up to 4 days.

Prep time: 10 minutes
Cook time: 0 minutes
Cool time: 20 minutes

eggnog popcorn

SERVES: 6

Eggnog is one of my husband's favorite holiday treats. Fortunately, eggnog-flavored instant pudding mix, which is available seasonally, makes creating eggnog-flavored popcorn no problem at all. Whip up a batch of this popcorn in thirty minutes or less and enjoy the season.

8 cups popped popcorn (see page 7)
1 cup white chocolate or vanilla melting candy (see page 11)
1 tablespoon eggnog-flavored instant pudding mix
⅛ teaspoon ground cinnamon
⅛ teaspoon ground nutmeg

Pour the popcorn into a large bowl and remove any unpopped kernels.

Place the white melting candy in a medium microwave-safe bowl. Microwave on medium power for 1 minute. Stir until melted and smooth. If needed, add additional heating time in 30-second increments, stirring after each time, until the candy is melted and smooth. Whisk the pudding mix, cinnamon, and nutmeg into the melting candy.

Pour the melted candy over the popcorn. Using a large rubber spatula, gently stir to coat.

Spread the popcorn mixture on a large piece of parchment paper or a large silicone baking mat.

Allow to cool until the candy coating has hardened, about 20 minutes. Break into pieces before packaging or transferring to a bowl to serve immediately. The popcorn may be stored in an airtight container for up to 4 days.

Prep time: 10 minutes
Cook time: 0 minutes
Cool time: 20 minutes

acknowledgments

Writing this book truly taught me the meaning of the phrase, "it takes a village." I would have never guessed what a massive team effort lies behind the publication of a cookbook before I embarked on this adventure! There are so many of you who made this book possible. I may not be able to thank each and every one of you by name here in print, but please know that your support has been noticed and invaluable to me.

I so appreciate the enormous time and effort put forth towards this project by Holly Schmidt, Justin Schwartz, and Cindy Brzostowski. They exerted a tremendous amount of patience and taught me how to write a cookbook.

Thank you to my sweet husband, Chris, for all the hours you spent taking on my day-to-day mothering and homemaking tasks in addition to the full load you already bear. I couldn't survive a day without you.

Thank you to Aunt Addy for taking an entire week out of her vacation time to come play Mom to my daughter around the clock while I went to the library to write.

Thank you to Aunt L who always had open arms and an open heart to offer my sweet girl when I wasn't there.

Thank you to my little Emma for letting me go without tears when I needed quiet time to write; for jumping into my arms when I came back. And thank you for loving popcorn. It was fun for me to create something I knew you would appreciate one day.

Thank you to my Mom and Dad. I've appreciated how excited you've been for me to have this experience. Your selflessness and genuine interest in the things that are important to me have been the ultimate example I wish to follow as a parent.

Thank you to Caleb, Keaton, Cooper, and Casey simply for being my brothers. You deserve a spot on the acknowledgements page.

Thank you to Tammy for your continued enthusiasm for this project.

And finally: thank you to my Something Swanky (www.something swanky.com) family. This book would have never (in a million years) been possible without the support of my readers and the blogging community encouraging me and cheering me on. Special thanks to Dorothy, Christi, Averie, Aimee, and Camille who all talked me off the ledge at one point or another in this crazy cookbook-writing process.

index